Samuel Johnson's Critical Opinions

A Reexamination

Arthur Sherbo

DELAWARE

Newark: University of Delaware Press
London: Associated University Presses

Associated University Presses
440 Forsgate Drive
Cranbury, NJ 08512

Associated University Presses
25 Sicilian Avenue
London WC1A 2QH, England

Associated University Presses
P.O. Box 338, Port Credit
Mississauga, Ontario
Canada L5G 4L8

The paper used in this publication meets the requirements
of the American National Standard for Permanence of Paper
for Printed Library Materials Z39.48-1984.

Library of Congress Cataloging-in-Publication Data

Sherbo, Arthur, 1918–
    Samuel Johnson's critical opinions : a reexamination / Arthur Sherbo.
        p.   cm.
    Includes bibliographical references and index.
    ISBN 0-87413-547-8 (alk. paper)
    1. Johnson, Samuel, 1709–1784—Knowledge—Literature.
2. Shakespeare, William, 1564–1616—Criticism and interpretation—
Quotations, maxims, etc.   3. Literature—History and criticism—
Quotations, maxims, etc.   4. Criticism—England—Quotations,
maxims, etc.   5. Johnson, Samuel, 1709–1784—Quotations.   I. Title.
PR3537.L5S54   1995
828'.609—dc20   94-43846
                                                                          CIP

PRINTED IN THE UNITED STATES OF AMERICA

For Irene,

coadjutor
and
expediter

Contents

Abbreviations

Greene	*Samuel Johnson's Library: An Annotated Guide,* ed. Donald J. Greene, *English Literary Studies Monographs,* University of Victoria, B.C., Canada, 1975.
Hazen	Allen T. Hazen, *Samuel Johnson's Prefaces and Dedications,* New Haven, 1937.
JEB	Brown, Joseph Epes, *The Critical Opinions of Samuel Johnson,* Princeton, 1926.
J. Misc.	*Johnsonian Miscellanies,* ed. G. B. Hill, 2 vols. Oxford, 1897.
Lennox	Charlotte Lennox, *Shakespear Illustrated,* 3 vols., London, 1753–54.
Letters	*The Letters of Samuel Johnson,* ed. R. W. Chapman, 3 vols. Oxford, 1952.
Life	James Boswell, *Life of Johnson,* ed. G. B. Hill, rev. and enlarged by L. F. Powell, 6 vols. Oxford, 1934–50.
Lit. Anecd.	John Nichols, *Literary Anecdotes of the Eighteenth Century,* 9 vols. 1812–15.
Lives	*Lives of the English Poets,* ed. G. B. Hill, 3 vols. Oxford, 1905.
P.P.	*Private Papers of James Boswell . . . ,* ed. Geoffrey Scott and F. A. Pottle, 18 vols. Privately printed, New York, 1928–50.
Piozzi/Shaw	Hester Lynch Piozzi, *Anecdotes of Samuel Johnson* and William Shaw, *Memoirs of Dr. Johnson,* ed. A. Sherbo, Oxford, 1974.
Reade	Aleyn Lyell Reade, *Johnsonian Gleanings: Part V: The Doctors's Life, 1728–1735,* privately printed, London, 1928.
Wks.	*Works of Samuel Johnson,* ed. F. P. Walesby, 9 vols. Oxford, 1825.
Yale	Yale edition of the *Works of Samuel Johnson,* various editors, New Haven and London, various dates. The various works are identified in the text. Vols. 7 and 8 are Johnson on Shakespeare.

Samuel Johnson's
Critical Opinions

Introduction

Joseph Epes Brown's *The Critical Opinions of Samuel Johnson* was published by the Princeton University Press in 1926 and reprinted without change in 1961 by Russell and Russell, Inc. of New York. At the time I write (1993) some sixty-five years have passed since the original publication, a period that has seen great advances in Johnsonian studies. The time has come for a reexamination of Johnson's critical opinions in the light of these advances, most notably the Hill-Powell edition of Boswell's *Life* of Johnson, R. W. Chapman's edition of Johnson's letters, and the volumes of the Yale edition of Johnson's works. One immediately observable shortcoming of JEB is the reliance on Walter Raleigh's *Johnson on Shakespeare* (1915, hereafter Raleigh) for Johnson's critical opinions on Shakespeare rather than on the actual editions of Shakespeare edited by Johnson and by Johnson with George Steevens. Raleigh prints only a very few of the notes on the plays, omitting countless others. And while JEB lists the 1765 *Shakespeare* edited by Johnson as one source for the critical opinions, only three (numbers 18, 40, 57) of the 157 entries in the thirty-six pages devoted to Shakespeare are to that edition. While a number of these entries refer to others of Johnson's writings on Shakespeare, the very great majority of them are to Raleigh. No account is taken of the 1773, 1778, and 1785 editions of Shakespeare edited by Johnson and Steevens. Those critical opinions expressed in some of the eighty-four new notes Johnson added to the 1773 edition are not, of course, included in JEB. Nor is the striking sentence added to the preface in the 1778 edition: "What he [Shakespeare] does best, he soon ceases to do." Many years ago I wrote,

> An unwillingness to realize that the edition of Shakespeare is probably only second to the *Lives of the Poets* in its importance for our understanding of Johnson's criticism in operation, and that that importance resides primarily in the notes, has caused too many critics to labor *in vacuo*. Does one wish to learn what Johnson thought of particular lines, situations, and soliloquies in Shakespeare's plays? Let him turn to the commentary, for he certainly will not find this information

13

in the Preface. Is the reader curious to discover Johnson's views on Shakespeare's imagery, his appreciation of Shakespeare's art and his "blind spots?" Let him read the notes to Shakespeare.[1]

This holds true today, and is of especial importance for any detailed discussion of Johnson's critical opinions. I defer discussion of Johnson's further critical opinions about Shakespeare for later treatment.

Professor Brown states in his preface that "No attempt has been made to preserve entire Johnson's emendatory criticism of Shakespeare, or comment on particular passages. Only such notes have been quoted as seem to illuminate his critical principles, or his appreciation—or lack of appreciation—of Shakespeare" (p. viii). With all due respect, this will not do. Brown quotes and cites from the *Lives* to considerable extent; the Shakespeare edition, rarely consulted, has been slighted. And yet Johnson devoted more of his critical attention and, indeed of his time, to Shakespeare than to any other writer. Raleigh reprints the concluding remarks on each of Shakespeare's plays, remarks which are well known as General Observations. He notes at one point in his introduction that Johnson "never took kindly to the labours of revision; and his first edition remains the authorative text of his criticism" (p. xiv), a statement which later scholarship has shown to be entirely mistaken. Among the new material in the 1773 Johnson-Steevens edition are the General Observations on *The Tempest,* the first sentence of which had appeared as a note in the 1765 Appendix; and that on *The Merry Wives of Windsor.* That on *A Midsummer Night's Dream* was originally a note in the 1765 appendix, being removed to the end of the play in 1773. Additionally, the second paragraph of that on *Titus Andronicus* was added in 1773. Raleigh does include the Observations on *A Midsummer Night's Dream* and on *Titus Andronicus,* but not those on *The Tempest* and *The Merry Wives of Windsor.*

Professor Brown states that Johnson's "Shakespeare criticism now seems strangely insensible to the more poetical qualities of the dramatist" (p. xxxv), a statement made possible by the neglect of the commentary on the plays resulting from his reliance upon the selection of notes in Raleigh's *Johnson on Shakespeare.* Johnson's appreciation of the "poetical qualities of the dramatist" will, however, be seen below in the notes on the plays. What is more, Johnson wrote in the preface to his edition, "The poetical beauties or defects I have not been very diligent to observe. Some plays have more, and some fewer judicial observations, not in proportion to their difference of merit, but because I gave this part of the design to chance and to caprice. The reader, I believe, is seldom pleased to find his opinion anticipated, it is natural to delight more in what we find or make, than in what we receive" (Yale 7:104). Despite this statement, he could not help observing poetical beauties as well as defects.

I have made a few departures from JEB, some of them in the nature of additions. Thus, I have included the names of two actors and one actress, about whom Johnson had something to say by way of criticism. I have not introduced many new topics, as opposed to writers and their works. "Music" and "Restoration wits" come to mind. JEB has "English Language" as a topic; I have added "Language." Incidentally, the topics in JEB are under the heading "Principles of Criticism," but nowhere is there a definition of what a "critical opinion" actually is. Possibly no exact definition is needed, so that Johnson's recommending a work may be thought a critical opinion. Since JEB is the pioneer work and so much of the ground has been covered, I have allowed myself to quote Johnson's opinions somewhat more *in extenso* than was possible for Professor Brown. I have quoted where JEB merely cited, i.e., a reference to *Lives* without any quotation now appears with the quoted opinion. This has resulted in a more readily accessible compilation, the various works by Johnson not usually at hand for users of this work. Sometimes JEB will quote a critical opinion in the topics section, naming the writer, but will not include that writer in the authors and their works section. Thus, Johnson is quoted, under "Travel, Books of," on Dr. Edward Browne's book of travels (not otherwise identified), but there is no entry for Dr. Browne in the other section. I have included him there. So, too, with Walter Haddon, who is linked with Roger Ascham in the fourth entry under Ascham in JEB but who has no separate entry for the statement linking him with Ascham. I have also allowed myself to add an occasional note to my entries and to expand a mere reference to a critical opinion by quotation of that opinion. Thus, as but one example, the second entry under Abraham Cowley in JEB reads: "The genius of C. referred to *Wks.* 5. 36, 37 (*Ramb.* 6) 1750." What the user of JEB would not know without going to the *Rambler* is that Johnson was referring in the first passage (36) to a particular work of Cowley's, for he wrote of his "remembrance of a passage in Cowley's preface to his poems, where, however exalted by genius and enlarged by study." The *second* passage (37) cited contains the words "the genius of Cowley." As will have been noted I give reference to the

Yale edition of Johnson's works, the passage I quote being at 3:32. And see under Cowley below, a critical opinion overlooked in JEB.

I have come upon a few errors in JEB. On page 452 one finds "*Rabelais, Francois*. 1. 'The licentious *Rabelais*' ridicules the superstitions of astrology 'with exquisite address and humour.' *Shak.*, Raleigh, 156." Recourse to page 156 of Raleigh reveals that the reference is to Edmund's speech in *King Lear,* beginning "This is the excellent foppery of the world," which occasioned a long note, some two-and-a-half pages in Raleigh, in which the words quoted in JEB appear and in which there is also a passing reference to "the great Milton," also enshrined in JEB. The truth of the matter is that the note is unsigned in Johnson's 1765 *Shakespeare* and hence presumably by him. Had Raleigh consulted the 1773 Johnson-Steevens *Shakespeare* he would have found the note properly attributed to William Warburton in whose 1747 *Shakespeare* it appeared (IV.20,9).[2] Therefore "the exquisite address and humour" was Warburton's. What is more, Johnson never expressed a critical opinion about Rabelais. The mistaken attribution was perpetuated in *Johnson. Prose and Poetry* (1950), edited by Mona Wilson and John Crow. Delete the Rabelais item and "the great Milton" from JEB. JEB notes that a critical remark on the diction of John Gower comes from the "History of the English Language" in Johnson's *Dictionary.* The remark is on Chaucer's diction, not Gower's (see Chaucer below). There is no entry in JEB for Robert Blair, author of *The Grave,* a poem wrongly attributed to Hugh Blair (p. 287). And there is a minor error, Mme. Du Boccage being denied one "c" in her name.

The user of this revised JEB, the revision being, as has been noted, in the addition of some four hundred new notes and some one hundred and thirty authors and works, now really has Johnson's critical opinions on Shakespeare's plays. One can now see Johnson's blind spots, what he could not "understand," what he found "obscure," what he found "corrupted." One can, of course, also see what Johnson admired in the plays—a scene, a passage, a single word, an image. And one will see Johnson the man in the edition,[3] as witness this note on *Measure for Measure,* at the juncture where the disguised Duke speaks to Claudio:

> Thou hast nor youth, nor age;
> But as it were an after-dinner's sleep
> Dreaming on both

                                        (III, i, 32)

Johnson comments,

> This is exquisitely imagined. When we are young we busy ourselves in forming schemes for succeeding time, and miss the gratifications that are before us; when we are old we amuse the langour of age with the recollection of youthful pleasures or performances; so that our life, of which no part is filled with the business of present time, resembles our dreams after dinner, when the events of the morning are mingled with the designs of the evening.

This is not the only note in which Johnson comments on Shakespeare and upon life in general, as well as upon some aspect of his own life and thought.

Largely because of the addition of some one hundred thirty names of authors and works one can now realize the extent to which Johnson, a writer of sermons and of a book of travels, read, reflected upon, and pronounced upon the sermons and books of travels of other authors. That he read widely is of course well known, and I have noted, when pertinent, the books he possessed of the authors about whom and whose works he offered critical opinions. There are extant catalogues of the books he had as a student at Pembroke College, Oxford and of those that were sold at his death. And yet there are among the further critical opinions which I have gathered remarks on authors and works which make but the one appearance in the whole canon of his works and conversation.

Finally, I introduce "Puppy" as a critical term. Dr. Edward Harwood's *Liberal Translation of the New Testament* fell into Johnson's hands. He glanced at it, saw that Harwood had translated "Jesus wept" as "Jesus, the Saviour of the world, burst into a flood of tears," and, contemptuously throwing the book aside, exclaimed "Puppy!" This is but a foretaste of the treat that is in store for admirers of Johnson, as well as for admirers of good literary criticism. Close students of Johnson's literary criticism and especially of his Shakespearian criticism will observe the occurrence, in many of the quoted notes, of the terms of his critical vocabulary—harsh, mean, licentious, natural, elegant, congruous, proper—to name but a few. Since Johnson had opinions about act and scene beginnings and endings I have included his notes on this aspect of Shakespeare criticism.

In the section devoted to Shakespeare's plays, act, scene and line references are to the Riverside *Shakespeare* edited by G. Blakemore Evans (1974), as those in Johnson's editions are based on other than modern criteria. Since I quote only enough of Shakespeare's text, usually only the first lines of a long passage, and only the critical part of Johnson's notes, I have given volume and page number of Johnson's *Shakespeare* (1765 and 1773) for those fortunate enough to have either of those editions, that they may see the whole passage in Shakespeare and the whole of Johnson's note. So, too, for those who have volumes 7 and 8 of the Yale edition of Johnson's works to which reference is made in what follows. Recourse to the Riverside *Shakespeare* will give the entire passage in Shakespeare, although allowance must of course be made for textual differences. All references are to Johnson's 1765 Shakespeare unless otherwise identified. J = Johnson; some of J's works are abbreviated in easily identifiable form, *Pref. to S.*, *Hist. Eng. Lang. Dict*, *Plan of Dict.*, *Proposals* (i.e., *Proposals for Printing the Works of Shakespeare*), *Adv.* (*Adventurer*), *Ramb.* (*Rambler*).[4]

I am sure other scholars will find critical opinions I have overlooked. May I suggest they send them to the *Johnson News Letter.*

NOTES

1. *Samuel Johnson, Editor of Shakespeare* (Urbana, 1956), p. 62.

2. It may be well to add that a note on *A Midsummer Night's Dream*, attributed to J by Raleigh (pp. 68–69), is also by Warburton. See volume 1, page 109, note 3 of his edition of Shakespeare (1747).

3. See my article "Johnson's *Shakespeare*, The Man in the Edition," *College Literature*, 17 (1990): 53–64.

4. I have not seen fit to discriminate among the many modern attributions of various works to Johnson, being increasingly aware of the uncertainty of these attributions. I have made but one exception: Allen T. Hazen's *Samuel Johnson's Prefaces and Dedications* (New Haven, 1937) from which I have accepted three attributions.

Critical Opinions

Entries with an asterisk (*) do not appear in JEB.

ADDISON, JOSEPH

"The excellent Mr. Addison's 'Moral and Religious Essays' praised for their morality and religiosity" *Preceptor, Wks.*, 5:244

"what voice or gesture can help to add dignity or force to the soliloquy of Cato?" *Pref. to S.*, Yale, 7:79

A Letter from Italy, ll. 113, 117–18
Addison "has been with justice accused of a solecism in this passage:

> The poor inhabitant—
> Starves in the midst of nature's bounty curst,
> And in the loaden vineyard *dies of thirst—*"
> *Plan of Dict., Wks.*, 5:13

J is quoted on ll. 174–80, "I bridle in my struggling muse with pain / That longs to launch into a nobler strain," to the effect that it was "a broken metaphor between riding and sailing, neither of which were, he said, applicable to the muse." Hester Lynch Piozzi, *British Synonymy* (1794, II.377–78). See also *Lives,* 2:128 for a slightly different version.
[J had, however, high praise for the *Letter from Italy* in the life of Addison, *Lives,* 2:86, 128.]

Spectator 285
Addison was "unsuccessful in enumerating the ways with which Milton has enriched our language." Yale, 7:54

Spectator 517
"Addison killed Sir Roger, that no other hand might attempt to exhibit him." Yale, 8:542

Tatler 117
"Addison, who has remarked, with a poor attempt at pleasantry,

that 'he who can read it [the description of Dover cliffs in *King Lear*] without being giddy has a very good head, or a very bad one.'" Yale, 8:695

[J had Addison's *Miscellaneous Works*, 4 volumes. Reade, p. 226.]

ALEXANDRINE

An "alexandrine with the addition of two syllables, is no more an alexandrine than with the detraction of the syllables." Review of Joseph Warton's *Essay on the Writings and Genius of Pope*, *Wks.*, 6:45

"It is now only used to diversify heroick lines." "Grammar of the English Tongue" in his *Dict.* (sig. d.)

The "measure" of *Robert of Gloucester*, "however rude and barbarous it may seem, taught the way to the *Alexandrine* of the *French* poetry." *Hist. Eng. Lang. Dict.* (E2r)

"The alexandrine was, I believe, first used by Spenser, for the sake of closing his stanza with a fuller sound." *Lives*, 1:466

"The English alexandrine breaks the lawful bounds, and surprises the reader with two syllables more than he expected." *Lives*, 1:466

ANACHRONISM

A "late writer [Johnson in *Irene*] has put Harvey's doctrine of the circulation of the blood into the mouth of a Turkish statesman, who lived near two centuries before it was known even to philosophers or anatomists." *Ramb.* 140, Yale, 4:377

ARIOSTO

"Dr. Johnson said, that no poet could *invent* a series or combination of incidents the praecognito of which might not be found in Homer; and should we claim an exception or two in favour of Shakespeare and Ariosto, those exceptions would prove the rule." Hester Lynch Piozzi, *British Synonymy* (1794) II.331–32

[J had editions of Ariosto in Italian and John Hoole's English translation of 1783. Greene, p. 30.]

ARISTOTLE

"He [J] used to quote, with great warmth, the saying of Aristotle . . . that there was the same difference between the learned and unlearned, as between the living and the dead." *Life*, 4:13

ASTLE, THOMAS*

The Will of King Alfred (published 1788)
"Your notes on Alfred appear to me very judicious and accurate but they are too few." *Letters*, 2:432

ATTERBURY, BISHOP FRANCIS*

Sermons
"One of the best . . ." *Life*, 3:247

AUTHORS

"No expectation is more fallacious than that which authors form of the reception which their labours will find among mankind." Preface to *Rolt's Dictionary of Trade and Commerce*, *Wks.*, 5:247

"The reciprocal civility of authors is one of the most risible scenes in the farce of life." *Life of Sir Thomas Browne*, *Wks.*, 6:478–79

BACON, SIR FRANCIS

See Language*.

BAILLET, ADRIEN*

Jugemens des Scavans
"His catalogue [of the prejudices which mislead the critick . . .]

though large, is imperfect, and who can hope to complete it?" *Ramb.* 93, Yale, 4:130

"Of the celebrated printers you do not [need] to be informed, and if you did, you might consult Baillet's Jugemens des Scavans." *Letters,* 1:218

BARBAULD, ANNA LETETIA*

Hymns in Prose for Children
"Mrs. Barbauld had however his best praise, and deserved it; no man was more struck than Mr. Johnson with voluntary descent from possible splendour to painful duty." Piozzi/Shaw, pp. 65–66

"Too much is expected of precocity, and too little performed. Miss -[Aiken, later Mrs. Barbauld] was an instance of early cultivation, but in what did it terminate?"

[The identification of Miss Aiken is made in a note on the passage in the *Life,* 2:408, n. 1. Mrs. Barbauld helped her husband in "an infant boarding school."]

BARCLAY, ALEXANDER*

His *Eglogues* "are probably the first in our language." *Life,* 1:277

BARRETIER, JEAN PHILIPPE*

"Barretier, whose early advances in literature scarce any human mind has equalled." *Adv.* 39, Yale, 2:347

Barretier's notes to his translation of "the travels of rabbi Benjamin" afford "many instances of penetration, judgment, and accuracy." *Life of Barretier, Wks.,* 6:378

BARROW, DR. ISAAC*

Hawkins heard J declare his sentiments on various works of "divines and other of the past century." He admired Hooker for "his logical precision," Sanderson "for his acuteness, and Taylor

for his amazing erudition; Sir Thomas Browne for his penetration, and Cowley for the ease and unaffected structure of his periods. The tinsel of Sprat disgusted him, and he could but just endure the smooth verbosity of Tillotson. Hammond and Barrow he thought involved, and of the latter that he was unnecessarily prolix." Sir John Hawkins, *Life of Samuel Johnson*, Dublin, 1787, p. 241
[J] had a four-volume edition of Barrow's works. Greene, p. 33.]

BARRY, SPRANGER (ACTOR)*

"Johnson said that he [Barry] was fit for nothing but to stand at an auction room door with his pole." Dr. Thomas Campbell's *Diary of a Visit to England in 1775*, ed. J. L. Clifford, 1947, p. 97
[Barry played the part of Mahomet in J's *Irene*.]

BAXTER, REV. RICHARD*

Boswell asked which of Baxter's works to read: "Read any of them; they are all good." *Life*, 4:226

"Baxter's 'Reasons of the Christian Religion,' he thought contained the best collection of the evidences of the divinity of the Christian system." *Life*, 4:237

BEHN, APHRA

Perhaps if skill could distant times explore,
New Behns, new Durfeys, yet remain in store.
"Drury-Lane Prologue," *Poems*, Yale, 6:89

BELLAMY, MRS. GEORGE ANNE (ACTRESS)*

"'Cleone' was well acted by all the characters, but Bellamy left nothing to be desired." *Life*, 1:325

BENTLEY, RICHARD

"You have, perhaps, no man who knows as much Greek and Latin as Bentley." *Life*, 4:217

Editor, *Paradise Lost,* 1732

Bentley "unhappily praised him [Milton] as introducer of those elisions in poetry, which had been used from the first essays of versification among us." *Pref. to S.,* Yale, 7:54

[J had Bentley's editions of Horace, Manilius, and Terence. Greene, pp. 69, 81, and 109.]

BEVERIDGE, BISHOP WILLIAM*

J praised his sermons and those of Tillotson and Sherlock: *"there you drink the cup of salvation to the bottom." J Misc.,* 2:429

BIBLE*

Asked which commentary on the bible to read: "I would recommend Lowth and Patrick on the Old Testament, Hammond on the New." *Life,* 3:58

BIOGRAPHY

He instanced the Chaplain of the late Pearce, Bishop of Rochester, "whom he was to assist in writing some Memoirs of that Prelate, but who could tell almost nothing." *P.P.,* 11:174. See also *Life,* 2:446 and Derby, John, below.

[J had an edition of Zachary Pearce, Bishop of Rochester's *Commentary . . . on the Four Evangelists . . .,* edited by his chaplain John Derby, and with a life of Pearce largely written by Johnson himself. Greene, p. 90.]

If a man "profess to write a life, he must give it as it really was, and when I objected the danger of telling that Parnel was a drunkard, he [J] said that it would produce the instructive caution to avoid drinking when it was seen that even the learning and genius of Parnel could be debased by it." [Also] "a man's intimate friend should mention his faults if he writes his life." *P.P.,* 13:25; cf. *Life,* 3:155 for slightly different wording.

BIRCH, THOMAS

History of the Royal Society of London
"This book might, more properly, have been entitled by the

author, a diary rather than a history, as it proceeds regularly from day to day." J's review of Birch's *History of the Royal Society of London* in the *Literary Magazine, Wks.,* 6:76
[J owned a copy of volume 1 of this work. Greene, p. 38.]

BLACKMORE, SIR RICHARD

J of a blunder of Blackmore: "a blunder . . . will not be reckoned decisive against a poet's reputation." *J Misc.,* 2:314
[J had a copy of Blackmore's *Creation, a Philosophical Poem.* Greene, p. 227.]

BLAINVILLE, HENRI MARIE DUCROTAY DE*

Travels through Holland, etc., Translated from the French. See Twiss, Richard.

BLAIR, HUGH, DR.

"I have read over Dr. Blair's first sermon with more than approbation; to say it is good, is to say too little." *Life,* 3:97

"If they [Blair's sermons] are all like the first . . ., they are *sermones aurei, ac auro magis aurei.* It is excellently written both as to doctrine and language." *Life,* 3:104

"The Scotch write English wonderfully well." *Life,* 3:109

"I love 'Blair's Sermons.'" *Life,* 4:98
[J had two volumes of Blair's Sermons. Greene, p. 39.]

BLAIR, ROBERT*

The Grave
JEB (p. 287) mistakenly attributes the poem *The Grave* to Hugh Blair and notes that "J did not like it much." *Life,* 3:47

BOERHAAVE, DR. HERMAN*

"These are the writings of the great Boerhaave, which have made all encomiums useless and vain, since no man can attentively peruse them without admiring the abilities, and reverencing the virtue of the author." *Life of Boerhaave, Wks.*, 6:292

Boileau-Despreaux, Nicolas

Boileau "justly remarks" that "books which have stood the test of time" have "a better claim to our regard than any modern can boast." *Ramb.* 92, Yale, 4:122

Bolingbroke, Henry St. John, First Viscount

Of the edition of his works edited by David Mallet.
"Sir, he was a scoundrel and a coward: a scoundrel, for charging a blunderbuss against religion and morality; a coward, because he had not resolution to fire it off himself, but left half a crown to a beggarly Scotchman, to draw the trigger after his death." *Life,* 1:268

Boswell, James

Letter to the People of Scotland
"Your paper contains very considerable knowledge of history and of the constitution, very properly produced and applied." *Letters,* 3:137

Browne, Dr. Edward*

A Brief Account of Some Travels . . .
J could not recommend his book of travels "as likely to give much pleasure to common readers: for . . . a great part of his book seems to contain very unimportant accounts of his passage from one place where he saw little, to another where he saw no more." *Life of Sir Thomas Browne, Wks.*, 6:493

Browne, Isaac Hawkins*

"a friend of great eminence in the learned and the witty world . . ." *Letters,* 3:57

Browne, Moses*

Sunday Thoughts
"Johnson, who often expressed his dislike of religious poetry, and

who, for the purpose of religious meditation, seemed to think one day as proper as another, read these with cold approbation, and said, he had a good mind to write and publish *Monday Thoughts.*" *Lit. Anecd.,* 5:51

BROWNE, SIR WILLIAM*

The king to Oxford sent his troops of horse,
For Tories own no argument but force;
With equal care to Cambridge books he sent,
For Whigs allow no force but argument.

"one of the happiest extemporaneous productions he [J] ever met with."
Piozzi/Shaw, p. 73

BRUNI, LEONARDO, OF AREZZO ("LEONARDUS ARETINUS")*

Latin translation of "Aristotle's *Politicks.*"
"Much is due to those who first broke the way to knowledge, and left only for their successors the task of smoothing it." *Journey to the Western Islands of Scotland,* 1775, ed. J. D. Fleeman (1985), p. 11 and n. 4 on p. 159

BRYDONE, PATRICK*

Tour Through Sicily and Malta
J said "if Brydone were more attentive to his Bible, he would be a good traveller." *Life,* 3:356. *See* Twiss, Richard.

BUCHANAN, GEORGE

"He [J] bid me [Boswell] read Buchanan's *History* in Latin." *P.P.,* 11:208

He imitated the "language and style" of the ancients "with so great success." *Harleian Library, Wks.,* 5:188

[J owned Buchanan's *Poemata* and the 1715 Edinburgh *Opera.* Greene, p. 42.]

BURKE, EDMUND

"I'm afraid Burke sacrificed every thing to his wit. 'Tis wrong to introduce Scripture thus ludicrously." *P.P.,* 6:96–97
[Boswell had mentioned Burke's using "scripture phrases."]

BURNEY, DR. CHARLES

A General History of Music . . .
It "evidently proved that the Author of it understood the Philosophy of music better than any man who had ever written on that subject." *J. Misc.,* 2:286

CAMBRIDGE, RICHARD OWEN*

The Intruder
"it was not happy. . ." *Life,* 4:523
[*The Intruder: in Imitation of Horace, Book I. Satire ix.* (1754). See *Life,* 3: 250–51 where J and Cambridge and others discuss Horace.]

CAMPBELL, DR. JOHN*

Hermippus Redivivus
"His 'Hermippus Redivivus' is very entertaining, as an account of the Hermetick philosophy, and as furnishing a curious history of the extravagancies of the human mind." *Life,* 1:417

"I think highly of Campbell. . . . he has very extensive reading . . . history, politicks, in short, that popular knowledge which makes a man very useful . . . he has learned much by what is called *vox viva.*" *Life,* 5:324

CARTER, MISS ELIZABETH

"She ought to be celebrated in as many different languages as Lewis le Grand." *Letters,* 1:11

"learn'd Eliza, sister of the Muse" *To Eliza Plucking Laurel in Mr. Pope's Gardens,* in *Poems,* Yale, 6:62
[J had Miss Carter's edition of Epictetus. Greene, p. 56.]

CAXTON, WILLIAM*

Translation of *Destruccion of Troye*
"a book . . . which, tho' now driven out of notice by authors of no greater use or value, still continued to be read in Caxton's English . . ." *Idler* 69, Yale, 2:215

His translations from the French "in which the original is so scrupulously followed, that they afford us little knowledge of our own language; tho' the words are English the phrase is foreign." *Idler* 69, Yale, 2:215

CHANDLER, RICHARD*

Travels in Asia Minor
"Do not buy Chandler's travels, they are duller than Twiss's." *Letters,* 2:32. *See* Twiss, Richard.

CHAUCER, GEOFFREY [MISTAKENLY UNDER GOWER, JOHN IN JEB]

His diction was "in general like that of his contemporaries; and some improvements he undoubtedly made by the various dispositions of his rhymes, and by the mixture of different numbers, in which he seems to have been happy and judicious." *Hist. Eng. Lang. Dict.* (F2r)

CHESTERFIED, PHILIP DORMER STANHOPE, 4TH EARL OF

"*All the celebrated qualities of Chesterfield,* (said Johnson to an intimate friend, to whom he was then in the habit of unbosoming himself on occasion) *are like certain species of fruit which is pleasant*

enough to the eye, but there is no tasting it without danger." Piozzi/
Shaw, pp. 25–26

CHEYNE, DR. GEORGE*

English Malady
J twice recommended his *English Malady, or a Treatise of Nervous
Diseases of All Kinds. Life,* 3:27, 87
[J had an edition of this work. Greene, p. 48.]

CHRYSOSTOM, ST.*

De Sacerdotio
"exhibits a scene of enchantments not exceeded by any romance
of the middle ages." *Miscellaneous Observations on the Tragedy of
Macbeth,* Yale, 7:4
[J had "Chrysostom's opera, Graec. 8t. Eton, 1612." Greene,
p. 49.]

CICERO

"the great Roman orator . . ." *Plan of Dict., Wks.,* 5:21
[J had copies of *De Officiis, Epistolae ad Familiares,* and *Epistolae ad
Atticum.* Greene, p. 223.]

CLARKE, DR. SAMUEL*

"the most complete literary character that England ever produced . . ." William Seward, *Anecdotes of Some Distinguished Persons* (1795–97), 2:397, quoted in *Life,* 1:3, n. 2

"I should recommend Dr. Clarke's sermons, were he orthodox."
Life, 3:248

"He pressed me [Dr. Richard Brocklesby] to study Dr. Clarke and
to read his Sermons. I asked him why he pressed Dr. Clarke,
an Arian. 'Because, (said he,) he is fullest on the *propitiary sacrifice.'" Life,* 4:416

"Of Dr. Clarke he spoke with great commendation for his Universality & seemed not disposed to censure him for his Heterodoxy." *Life,* 4:524

Queried as to the best sermons in the English language: "bating a little heresy those of Dr. Samuel Clarke . . ." *J Misc.,* 2:305
[J had two editions of Clarke's *Sermons.* Greene, p. 49.]

Cocchi, Dr. Antonio Celestino*

"one of the politest scholars in *Europe* . . ." *Some Account of a Book, Called the Life of Benvenuto Cellini. Wks.* (1816), 2:194 [Cocchi wrote much on matters medical.]

Composition

"Of composition there are different methods. Some employ at once memory and invention; and with little intermediate use of the pen, form and polish large masses by continued meditation, and write their productions only when, in their opinion, they have completed them." *Lives,* 3:218

Cowley, Abraham

Cowley's preface to his poems
"however excited by genius and enlarged by study . . ." *Ramb.* 6, Yale, 3:32
[JEB does not quote these words and does not identify the quotation as referring to Cowley's preface to his poems.]

"The celebrated stanza of Cowley, on a lady elaborately dressed, loses nothing of its freedom by the spirit of the sentiment."

Th' adorning thee with so much art
Is but a barb'rous skill,
'Tis like the pois'ning of a dart
Too apt before to kill.
The Waiting Maid, ll. 13–16. *Idler* 77, Yale, 2:241–42

[J had an edition of Cowley's Latin poems. Greene, p. 51.]

CRABBE, GEORGE

Dedication to *The Village*
"His Dedication will be least liked; it were better to contract it into a short sprightly Address." *Letters*, 3:10

CROFT, SIR HERBERT*

"He disapproved much of mingling real facts with fiction. On this account he censured a book entitled 'Love and Madness'" *Life*, 4:187
[*See* JEB, Fiction, no. 13, but he omits the second sentence and, hence, there is no mention of Croft.]
J "not pleased" with Croft's "Family Discourses." *Life*, 4:298

CROUSAZ, JEAN PIERRE DE

His commentary on Pope's *Essay on Man*
"He is far from deserving either indignation or contempt; . . . his notions are just, though they are sometimes introduced without necessity; and defended when they are not opposed; and that his abilities and parts are such as entitle him to reverence from those who think his criticism superfluous." *Controversy Between Mons. Crousaz and Mr. Warburton . . .*, *Wks.* 5:203

DEMOCRITUS*

"Once more, Democritus, arise on earth,
With cheerful wisdom and instructive mirth."
The Vanity of Human Wishes, ll. 49–50, *Poems*, Yale, 6:94.

Derby, John*

See Biography.

Diction

"Of the laborious and mercantile part of the people, the diction is in a great measure casual and mutable." *Pref. to Dict., Wks.,* 5:44

Dictionaries

"it is not enough that a dictionary delights the critick, unless, at the same time, it instructs the learner." *Pref. to Dict., Wks.,* 5:3

Dryden, John

Dryden "who mistakes genius for learning, and in confidence of his abilities, ventured to write of what he had not examined." *Hist. Eng. Lang. Dict.,* (F^v)

"Dryden well knew, had he been in quest of truth, that, in a pointed sentence, more regard is commonly had to the words than the thoughts, and that it is very seldom to be vigorously understood." Yale, 8:956

Dryden's "Essays and Prefaces" recommended as best for learning "the art of poetry . . ." *Preceptor, Wks.,* 5:240
[J owned a copy of the three-volume edition of Dryden's *Vergil,* his translation of Juvenal, and the *Fables.* Reade, p. 225.]

Durfey, Thomas*

Perhaps if skill could distant times explore,
New Behns, new Durfeys yet remain in store.
Drury-Lane Prologue, Poems, Yale, 6:89

[I believe this is the *only* mention of Durfey in the whole canon.]

EDWARDS, DR. EDWARD*

Emendations on Xenophon in *Memorabilia* (1785)
"Some of his emendations seem to me to [be] irrefragably certain, and such therefore as not to be lost." *Letters,* 3:180

EDWARDS, THOMAS

"This note of Mr. Edwards, with which I suppose no reader is satisfied, shews with how much greater ease critical emendations are destroyed than made, and how willingly every man would be changing the text, if his imagination would furnish alterations." Yale, 7:121
See Emendation.

He "has justly censured the misquotation of 'stall-worn' for 'stall-worth!'" Yale, 8:845

ELPHINSTON, JAMES

Translation of Martial (1772)
"There are in these verses . . . too much folly for madness, I think, and too much madness for folly." Piozzi/Shaw, p. 80

EMENDATION

"To change an accurate expression for an expression confessedly not accurate has something of retrogradation." Yale, 7:309
"An editor is not always to change what he does not understand." Yale, 7:457
See also, for some further examples, Yale, 8:576, 729, 762, 885, 963.

ESSEX, ROBERT DEVEREUX, SECOND EARL OF*

Of a passage in a letter written just before his execution
"with which every reader will be pleased, though it is so serious

and solemn that it can scarcely be inserted without reverence."
Yale, 8:736

EVANS, EVAN*

J read his *Some Specimens of Antient Welsh Bards* "with attention and
[was] very much pleased" with it. *Life*, 2:513

FABRICIUS, JOHANN ALBRECHT*

Catalogus Librorum Bibliotheca Latina
"even the learned Fabricius cannot completely instruct him [the
reader] in the early editions of the classic writers." *Harleian
Library, Wks.*, 5:182
[J had three editions of the *Bibliotheca*. Greene, p. 57.]

FAIRFAX, EDWARD*

Translation of Tasso
The "elegance of Fairfax" in his translation of Tasso . . . *Idler* 69,
Yale, 2:215
[J had projected a new edition of Fairfax's translation. *Life*, 4:381]

FARMER, DR. RICHARD*

Essay on the Learning of Shakespeare (1769)
Percy wrote: "I never saw him so pleased with any literary production
of modern date, before in my life. He speaks of it with
the most unreserved applause, as a most excellent per-
formance; as a compleat and finished piece that leaves
nothing to be desired in point of argument: For the
question is now forever decided." *The Percy Letters*, vol.
2, ed. D. Nichol Smith and Cleanth Brooks, 1946, p. 121

FAWKES, FRANCIS*

Translation of Anacreon's odes
"Frank Fawkes has done these very finely." Piozzi/Shaw, p. 75

[J had a copy of Fawkes's *Theocritus*. Greene, p. 109.]

FELTHAM, OWEN*

"Feltham appears to consider it as the established law of poetical translation, that the lines should be neither more nor fewer than those of the original." *Idler* 69, Yale, 2:216. *See* Translation.

FERGUSON, ADAM*

Essay on the History of Civil Society (1766)
"I do not . . . perceive the value of this new manner, it is only like Buckinger, who had no hands, and so wrote with his feet!" Piozzi/Shaw, p. 80

FICTION

"Fiction should not be introduced when there is a basis of truth." *P.P.*, 14:242

FLOYER, SIR JOHN*

Treatise on the Asthma
"His book by want of order is obscure." *Letters*, 3:185

FOOTE, SAMUEL*

"If Betterton were to walk into this room with Foote, Foote would soon drive him out of it." *Life*, 3:185

"There is a merriment in Foote which it is not easy to resist." *P.P.*, 11:285

FORBES, JOHN*

"Forbes wrote very well [in support of religion] but I believe he wrote before episcopacy was quite extinguished." *Life*, 5:252

[J owned a copy of Forbes's *Instructiones historico theologicae*. Greene, p. 59.]

FORDYCE, REV. DR. JAMES*

Sermons for Young Women
J "owned himself fond, he said, of a man, who notwithstanding his illiberality which still debased the literature of his country, had *no dirty heresies sticking about him*." Piozzi/Shaw, p. 42
[J had "a long and uninterrupted social connection with the Reverend Dr. James Fordyce." *Life,* 4:411.]

FORSTER, GEORGE*

Voyages to the South Seas
J found "a great affectation of fine writing in" his *Voyages to the South Seas,* adding, "he does not carry *me* along with him: he leaves me behind him; or rather, indeed, he sets me before him; for he makes me turn over many leaves at a time." *Life,* 3:180

FOSTER, DR. JAMES*

Sermons
"When M^rs. Thrale quoted something from Foster's Sermons he flew in a passion & said that Foster was a man of mean ability, & of no original thinking." *Dr. Campbell's Diary,* p. 54. Quoted in *Life,* 4:9, n. 5

GAY, JOHN

"Read Beggar's Opera, english rogue. Liked a thief better than before or since . . . I know not if *it has* made robbers, but *it has occasioned* such a LABEFACTION of principles; keep company with robber and *you* may be one." *P.P.*, 6:45. [Compare *Life*, 2:367.]

GENTLEMAN'S MAGAZINE*

"One of the most successful and lucrative pamphlets which literary history has upon record . . ." *Life of Edward Cave, Wks.*, 6:432

GOLDSMITH, OLIVER

"Madam [Mrs. Thrale], said he, *can you tell me how a man who shocks so much in company, can give so many charms to his writings?*" Piozzi/ Shaw, p. 56

J's Greek epitaph on him was translated into English by William Seward. *Anecdotes . . . 1798, II.466*. The Greek is printed in the *Life*, 2:282. Here is Seward's translation.

> Whoe'er thou art, with reverence tread
> Where Goldsmith's letter'd dust is laid.
> If nature and the historic page,
> If the sweet muse thy care engage,
> Lament him dead, whose powerful mind
> Their various energies combin'd.

[JEB does not quote either version.]

GOWER, JOHN

"The first of our authors, who can properly be said to have written *English*, was Sir *John Gower*." *Hist. Eng. Lang. Dict.*, (Fᵛ)

GRANGER, JAMES*

J declared his *Biographical History of England* (a short title) "full of curious anecdote, but might have been better done." *Life*, 5:255

GRAY, THOMAS

"I hate Gray and Mason, though I do not know them." *P.P.*, 10:177
[J had William Mason's edition of Gray's poems, 1775. Greene, p. 62.]

Green, Matthew*

The Spleen "is not poetry." *Life,* 3:38
[But J quoted a couplet from it to Boswell, *Life,* 3:405.]

Grey, Zachary

Critical, Historical, and Explanatory Notes on Shakespeare . . .
"Dr. Grey, whose diligent perusal of old English writers has en-
    abled him to make some useful observations. What he under-
    took he has well enough performed, but as he neither attempts
    judicial nor emendatory criticism, he employs rather his mem-
    ory than his sagacity." *Pref. to S,* Yale, 7:101
[*See* JEB, p. 367, where there is only the bare reference to
    Raleigh.]

"Such critics of Shakespeare as Theobald and [Zachary] Gray *[sic]*
    perceive matters that eluded Pope and Warburton." Yale, 7:101,
    n. 5

Haddon, Walter*

"Haddon was famous for his Latin style . . . but the first rude
    essays of authours compared with the works of their maturer
    years, are useful to shew how much is in the power of diligence."
    Life of Roger Ascham (1761), p. 53n. Quoted in *Life,* 1:551
[Linked with Ascham, Roger (JEB, p. 282) but not afforded a
    separate entry.]

Hailes, Sir David Dalrymple, Lord*

Of volume 1 of his *Annals of Scotland*
"His accuracy strikes me with wonder; his narrative is far superior
    to that of Henault." *Life* 2:421. *See* Henault.

"It is in our language . . . a new mode of history, which tells all that
    is wanted, and, I suppose, all that is known, without laboured
    splendour of language, or affected subtilty of conjecture . . . He
    seems to have the closeness of Henault without his constraint."
    Life, 2:383

"I looked very often into Henault; but Lord Hailes . . . leaves him
    far and far behind." *Life,* 2:412

Lord Hailes's *Annals* will "be a book that will always sell, it has such a stability of dates, certainty of facts, and punctuality of citation. I never before read scotch history with certainty." *P.P.*, 11:289

"Lord Hailes's 'Annals of Scotland' are very exact; but they contain dry particulars. They are to be considered as a Dictionary." *Life*, 3:404
[J had Dalrymple's *Annals of Scotland*, a work he helped the author revise. Greene, p. 52.]

HAMMOND, DR. HENRY*

"He was extremely fond of Dr. Hammond's Works, and sometimes gave them as a present to young men going into orders; he also bought them for the library at Streathem." *J Misc.*, 2:19. *See also* Barrow, Isaac.

J recommends his *Paraphrase and Annotations on the New Testament*. *Life*, 3:58
[J had a four-volume edition of Hammond's works (1684). Greene, p. 65.]

HANMER, SIR THOMAS

"Sir T. Hanmer, very acutely and judiciously, reads . . ." Yale, 7:248

"These three little speeches, which in other editions are only one, and given to Cleopatra, were happily disentangled by Sir T. Hanmer." Yale, 8:861

HANWAY, JONAS

"We are told much that might have been as well told without the journey. Digression starts from digression, and one subject follows another with or without connection." Notice of *Journal of an Eight Days Journey* in the *Literary Magazine* (Nov. 1756), *Wks.* (1816), 2:332

"We wish . . . he had submitted his pages to the inspection of a grammarian, that the elegances of one line might not have been disgraced by the improprieties of another." Review of the same book in the *Literary Magazine* (1757), *Wks.*, 6:20

HARDWICKE, PHILIP YORKE, FIRST EARL OF*

Spectator No. 364 was by him. J said "it was quite vulgar, and had nothing luminous." *Life*, 3:34

HARRIS, JAMES

Dedication to his *Hermes* . . .
"Though but fourteen lines long, there were six grammatical faults in it." Piozzi/Shaw, p. 80 .
[The dedication has thirty lines; the first page, *fourteen*, which, presumably, contained the six faults. J had a copy of *Hermes* . . . (1751). Greene, p. 65.]

HARTE, WALTER*

J "much commended him as a scholar," but "the defects in his history *[The History of Gustavus Adolphus]* proceeded not from imbecility, but from foppery." *Life*, 2:120

Harte's *Essays on Husbandry* "is good." *Life*, 4:78
[J had Harte's biography of Gustavus Adolphus. Greene, p. 65–66.]

HARWOOD, DR. EDWARD*

Literal Translation of the New Testament
Harwood's translation of "Jesus wept," i.e., "Jesus, the Saviour of the world, burst into a flood of tears," caused J to throw the book aside and exclaim "Puppy!" *Life*, 3:39, n. 1

HAY, WILLIAM*

Translation of Martial
Boswell showed J "a particular epigram" in Hay's translation of

Martial and thought "it was pretty well done." J said "No, it is *not* pretty well" and faulted the translation. *Life*, 5:368

HEATH, BENJAMIN*

Revisal of Shakespeare's Text (1765)
Heath "ridicules his [Shakespeare's] errors with airy petulance, suitable enough to the levity of the controversy." *Pref. to S.*, Yale, 7:100

"Every boy or girl finds the metre imperfect [in a passage in *Macbeth*] but the pedant [Heath] comes to the defense with a tribrachys or an anapaest, and sets it right at once by applying to one language the rules of another." Yale, 8:776
[J had a copy of the *Revisal*. Greene, p. 66.]

HENAULT, CHARLES JEAN FRANCOIS*

Nouvel Abrège Chronologique
See Hailes, Sir David Dalrymple, Lord.

HESIOD*

J quotes a line from *Hesiodi Fragmenta* and calls it "a noble line." It is translated as "Let youth in deeds, in counsel man engage; / Prayer is the proper duty of old age." *Life*, 5:63 and n. 1

HEXAMETER*

What thinge wants quiet and mery rest, endures but a small while. [From Ovid.]
"If this line was so translated when this treatise *[Toxophilus]* was first written in 1544, it is the oldest English hexameter that I remember." *The English Works of Roger Ascham*, ed. by James Bennet (1767), p. 64
[J was the actual editor of this work.]

HOADLY, BENJAMIN, DR.*

"I asked him if the *Suspicious Husband* did not furnish a well-drawn character, that of Ranger." 'No, Sir," said he, "Ranger is just a rake, a mere rake, and a lively young fellow, but no *character*.' *Life,* 2:50

HOGARTH, WILLIAM*

"The hand of art here torpid lies
        That traced th' essential form of grace,
Here death has clos'd the curious eyes
        That saw the manners in the face."
                "Epitaph on Hogarth," *Poems,* Yale, 6:268

HOLYDAY, OR HOLIDAY, BARTON

Notes on Juvenal
J "thought so highly of it as to have employed himself for some time translating them into Latin." *J Misc.,* 2:387
[JEB merely cites the above.]

HOMER

Odyssey
"If the exordial verses of Homer be compared with the rest of the poem, they will not appear remarkable for plainness or simplicity, but rather eminently adorned and illuminated." *Ramb.* 158, Yale, 5:79

"Homer has fewer passages unintelligible than Chaucer." *Pref. to S,* Yale, 7:110. *See* Ariosto.
[J had eight editions of Homer, none in translation. Greene, p. 69.]

HOOKER, RICHARD*

See Barrow, Isaac, and *see* Language.

HORACE

Of *Odes* III.xvi.9–16, as translated by Philip Francis, "Captains of ships to gold are slaves, / Though fierce as their own winds and waves."

"The close of this passage, by which every reader is now disappointed and offended . . ." *Adv.* 58, Yale, 2:374

Art of Poetry 40–41
"It is asserted by Horace that 'if matter be once got together, words will be found with very little difficulty'; a position which though sufficiently plausible to be inserted in poetical precepts, is by no means strictly and philosophically true." *Adv.* 138, Yale, 2:494–95
[J had eight editions of Horace in Latin (Greene, p. 69), the Delphin *Horace,* an unnamed English translation of the *Odes,* and an edition simply named "Horatius." Reade, pp. 215, 216, 222.]

HUME, DAVID

"a man who has so much conceit to tell all mankind that they have been bubled for ages and he is the wise man who sees better than they, and has so little scrupulosity as to venture to oppose those principles which have been thought necessary to human happiness. . . . I know not indeed whether he has first been a blockhead and that has made him a rogue, or first been a rogue and that has made him a blockhead." *P.P.,* 6:178

HURBERY, DR. MATTHEW*

Eighteen Sermons on Important Subjects (1774), posthumously published.
"Madam, I have been reading your late Husband's Sermons; they are excellent." *Lit. Anecd.* 9:560

IMAGINATION

"No Tragedy so strong on stage as alone. The effect all *imagination,* and when alone, nothing to confront it; whereas in Playhouse, see 'tis stage, not wild heath; Garrick, no Macbeth." *P.P.,* 9:265

"Appearance of Actor with whom I've drank tea counteracts imagination." *P.P.,* 7:273

JAMES I, KING OF ENGLAND*

"King James' theological knowledge was not inconsiderable." Yale, 8:524

JOHNSON, SAMUEL

"When I was a young man, I translated Addison's Latin poem on the Battle of the Pigmies and Cranes, and must plead guilty to the following couplet:

> Down from the guardian boughs the nests they flung,
> And killed the yet unanimated young.

And yet I trust I am no blockhead. I afterward changed *kill'd* into *crush'd.*" *Poems,* Yale, 6:22
[J had nineteen copies of his *Dict.,* his *Journey to the Western Islands,* and the three volumes of the *Lives.* Greene, pp. 72–73.]

JONES, SIR WILLIAM*

"Sir Wᵐ Jones he thought as splendid a literary character as any to be named." *Life,* 4:524

J "pronounced one day at my [Boswell's] house a most lofty panegyric upon Jones the Orientalist." *J Misc.,* 1:287

JONSON, BEN

Of the prologue and epilogue to *Henry VIII*
"It appears to me very likely that they were supplied by the friendship or officiousness of Jonson, whose manner they will be perhaps found exactly to resemble." Yale 8:658 [Modern opinion disagrees.]

[J had five volumes of Jonson's works, probably from the seven-volume edition by Peter Whalley. Greene, p. 73.]

JORTIN, DR. JOHN*

"*Jortin's* sermons are very elegant." *Life,* 3:248

J linked Jortin with Markland and Thirlby as "those contemporaries of great eminence." *Letters,* 2:514

Life of Erasmus: "a dull book." *J Misc.,* 2:12

JUNIUS, FRANCIS*

"Junius appears to have excelled in extent of learning, and Skinner in rectitude of understanding. Junius was accurately skilled in all the northern languages; Skinner probably examined the ancient and remoter dialects only by occasional inspection into dictionaries; but the learning of Junius is often of no other use than to show him a track, by which he may deviate from his purpose, to which Skinner always presses forward by the shortest way. Skinner is often ignorant, but never ridiculous: Junius is always full of knowledge, but his variety distracts his judgment, and his learning is very frequently disgraced by his absurdities." *Pref. to Dict., Wks.,* 5:29

[When asked how he was to get his etymologies for the *Dict.,* J replied, "Why, Sir, here is a shelf with Junius and Skinner and others." *Life,* 1:186.]

KELLY, HUGH

A Word to the Wise

> "—scenes unconscious of offense,
> —harmless merriment, or usefull sense

also "If want of skill, or want of care appear . . ." J's prologue to the play, *Poems,* Yale, 6:291

"A man who has written more than he has read . . ." *J Misc.,* 2:6
[J had two editions of Kelly's works. Greene, p. 74.]

KEYSLER, JOHANN GEORG*

Travels Through Germany, etc.
See Twiss, Richard.

LACOMBE, JACQUES*

Dictionnaire portatif des beaux-arts . . . Paris, 1752
J recommends it, as by "Abbé L'Avocat," confusing Lacombe, de-
scribed as "avocat" in the General Catalogue of the National
Library of France, with the Abbé Louis-François Lavocat. *J
Misc.,* 2:2

LANGUAGE

"From the authors which rose in the time of Elizabeth, a speech
might be formed adequate to all the purposes of use and elegance. If the language of theology were extracted from Hooker
and the translation of the Bible; the terms of natural knowledge
from Bacon; the phrases of policy, war, and navigation from
Raleigh; the dialect of poetry and fiction from Spenser and
Sidney; and the diction of common life from Shakespeare, few
ideas would be lost to mankind, for want of English words, in
which they might be expressed." *Plan. of Dict., Wks.,* 5:40

"He [Shakespeare] wrote at a time when our poetical language
was yet unformed, when the meaning of our phrases was yet in
fluctuation, when words were adopted at pleasure from the
neighbouring languages, and while the Saxon was still visibly
mingled in our diction." Yale, 7:53

"A language so ungrammatical as the English. . ." Yale, 7:55–56

"The coinage of new words is a violent remedy not to be used
but in the last necessity." Yale, 7:147

"Accidental and colloquial senses are the disgrace of language,
and the plague of commentators." Yale, 7:338

"It is impossible to fix the meaning of proverbial expressions."
Yale, 7:369

[On the inclusion of French words into the English language.]
"But when a word is to be admitted, the first question should
be, by whom was it ever received? in what book can it be read?
If it cannot be proved to have been in use, the reasons which
can justify its reception must be stronger than any critick will
often have to bring." Yale, 8:820

"If phraseology is to be changed as words grow uncouth by disuse,
or gross by vulgarity, the history of every language will be lost;
we shall no longer have the words of any authour." Yale, 8:966

"Language is only the instrument of science, and words are but
the signs of ideas." *Pref. Eng. Dict., Wks.*, 5:27

LE GRAND, JOACHIM*

"this learned dissertator . . . valuable for his industry and erudition . . ." Preface to *Father Lobo's Voyage to Abyssinia, Wks.*, 5:256

LELAND, DR. THOMAS*

History of Ireland from the Invasion of Henry II (1773)
"Dr. Leland begins his history too late." [with Henry II] *Letters*,
2:172

LENNOX, CHARLOTTE*

"The novel of Cynthio Giraldi, from which Shakespeare is supposed to have borrowed this fable [of *Measure for Measure*], may
be read in *Shakespear Illustrated* elegantly translated, with remarks which will assist the enquirer to discover how much absurdity Shakespeare has admitted or avoided." Yale, 7:215

"She has many fopperies, but she is a great Genius, and nullum
magnum ingenium sine mixtura, i.e., "great wit is sure to mad-

ness near allied." Seneca, de Tranquillitate, 17:10, Letters, 2:431–32

LIPSIUS, JUSTUS (JOEST LIPS)*

"The common voice of the multitude . . . in questions that relate to the heart of man, is . . . more decisive than the learning of Lipsius." Ramb. 52, Yale, 3:280

[J had eight volumes of Lipsius's works, and a copy of his Roma Illustrata. Greene, p. 77.]

LOCKE, JOHN*

On Locke's verse: "I know of none, sir [Boswell], but a kind of exercise prefixed to Dr. Sydenham's Works, in which he has some conceit about the dropsy, in which water and burning are united and how Dr. Sydenham removed fire by drawing off water, contrary to the usual practice . . ."

[Boswell, on page 94, writes that there was not one word of the conceit in Locke's verses, which he reprints, adding that the conceit was "the immediate invention of his (J's) own lively imagination."]

LOWTH, BISHOP ROBERT*

"all Scotland could not muster learning enough for Louth's [sic] prelections." Life, 5:57, n. 3

"Lowth is another bishop who has risen by his learning." Life, 5:81

"the late elegant productions of Bishop Lowth . . ." J Misc., 1:366

[J had Lowth's de sacra poesi Hebraeorum (the Praelectiones) and his translation of Isaiah. Greene, p. 78.]

LOWTH, DR. WILLIAM*

J recommends his Commentary on the Old Testament. Life, 3:58

LYDGATE, JOHN*

The Fall of Princes

J quotes a few stanzas out of the third book of The Fall, "which, being compared with the style of his two contemporaries [Gower and Chaucer], will show that our language was then not written by caprice, but was in a settled state." *Hist. Eng. Lang. Dict.*, (G[2]ʳ)

Lyttelton, George, First Baron

Observations on the Conversion and Apostleship of St. Paul
"Infidelity has never been able to fabricate a specious answer." *Lives*, 3:450 ["Specious" is defined in J's *Dict.* as "2. Plausible; superficially, not solidly right; striking at first view."]

Macaulay, Catharine Sawbridge*

"a female patriot bewailing the miseries of her 'friends and fellow-citizens.'" A reference to her *Address to the People of England, Scotland, and Ireland, on the Present Important Crisis of Affairs.* D. J. Greene, *Samuel Johnson Political Writings*, in Yale, 10:449, n.2
Boswell told J that he, J, had made her ridiculous. J replied, "That was already done, Sir. To endeavour to make *her* ridiculous, is like blacking the chimney." *Life*, 2.336

"It having been mentioned, I know not with what truth, that a certain female political writer, whose doctrines he disliked, had of late become very fond of dress, sat hours together at her toilet, and even put on rouge:—JOHNSON. 'She is better employed at her toilet, than using her pen. It is better she should be reddening her own cheeks, than blackening other people's characters.'" *Life*, 3:46
[J had two volumes of her *History of England*. Greene, p. 80.]

Machiavelli, Nicoló*

Discourse upon the first Decade of T. Livius
"Machiavel has justly animadverted on the different notice taken by all succeeding times, of the two great projectors Catiline and Caesar." *Adv.* 99, Yale, 2:430.

[J had his friend Guiseppe Baretti's edition of Machiavelli's works. Greene, p. 80.]

MALLET, DAVID

A Poem. In Imitation of Donaides.
"How false . . . is all this to say [as Mallet does] that in ancient times learning was not a disgrace to a peer as it is now. . . . I am always angry when I hear ancient times praised at the expense of modern times." *Life,* 4:217 and 520. *See* Bolingbroke.

MANDEVILLE, BERNARD DE

Treatise of Hyperchondriack and Hysteric Passions
J "thought highly" of it. *J Misc.,* 2:20

MARINI (OR MARINO), GIOVANNI BATTISTA*

"This kind of writing [metaphysical poetry], a high art, I believe borrowed from Marino and his followers. . ." *Lives,* "Cowley," 1:22

MARKLAND, JEREMIAH*

"He is a scholar undoubtedly . . . but remember he would run from the world, and that it is not the world's business to run after him." *Life,* 4:161, n.3. *See* Jortin, John.

MARRIOTT (OR MARRIOT), GEORGE*

The Jesuit, an ode
"Bolder words and more timorous meaning, I think were never brought together." *Life,* 4:13 and 477–78

MARTIN, MARTIN*

"No man now writes so ill as Martin's Account of the Hebrides [*Description of the Western Isles*] is written." *Life,* 3:243. J said he

read the book when "very young, and that he was highly pleased
with it." *Life*, 1:450

MASON, WILLIAM

"I hate Gray and Mason, though I do not know them." *P.P.*,
10:177.
[J had a Latin translation of Mason's play *Caractacus*. Greene,
p. 82.]

MATTAIRE (OR MAITTAIRE), MICHAEL*

"Mattaire's account of the Stephani [*Stephanorum Historia* . . .] is a
heavy book. He seems to have been a puzzle-headed man, with
a large share of scholarship, but with little geometry or logick
in his head, without method, and possessed of little genius."
Life, 4:2

"His book of the Dialects [*Graecae Linguae Dialecti* . . .] is a sad
heap of confusion." *Life*, 4:3
[J had Mattaire's *Miscellania graecorum aliquot Scriptorum Carmina*
(1722). Greene, p. 81.]

MERRYWEATHER, JOHN*

Translated *Religio Medici* into Latin "not inelegantly. . ." *Life of Sir
Thomas Browne, Wks.*, 6:480

METASTASIO, PIETRO*

"distinguished sometimes by graceful familiarity, and sometimes
by easy magnificence; his mien is soft, though his sentiments
are sublime. He mingles the wisdom of the politician with the
passion of his dialogues, and the precepts of the moralist with
the levity of his songs."
Dedication to *The Works of Metastasio*, by John Hoole (1767), in
Hazen, p. 68.

[J had an Italian edition of Metastasio's works as well as John Hoole's translation. Greene, p. 84.]

Milton, John

Paradise Lost
Mowbray in Shakespeare's *Richard II* says,

> Now no way can I stray,
> Save back to England; all the world's my way.

J comments, "Perhaps Milton had this in mind when he wrote these lines:

> The world was all before them, where to choose
> Their place of rest, and Providence their guide."
> [XII.646–47] Yale, 7:431

Lancaster, in *2 Henry IV*, says, "Between the grace, the sanctities of heav'n" and J comments, "This expression Milton has copied, 'Around him all the sanctities of Heav'n.'" [*Paradise Lost*, II.60] Yale, 7:511

Mortimer, in *1 Henry VI*, says, "Let dying Mortimer here rest himself." J writes, "I know not whether Milton did not take from this hint the lines with which he opens his tragedy 'A little onward lend this guiding hand / To these dark steps; a little further on.'" [*Samson Agonistes*, ll. 1–2] Yale, 8:571

Il Penseroso
Oberon, in *A Midsummer Night's Dream*, says

> Through this house give glimmering light,
> By the dead and drowsy fire
>
> [79–80]

J comments,
"Milton perhaps had this picture in his thought.

> Glowing embers through the room
> Teach light to counterfeit a gloom."
>
> Yale, 7:159

"*high, height,* which Milton, in zeal of analogy, writes *heighth . . .*"
Pref. to Dict., Wks., 5:25

J censures Milton's "miserable" equivocation in *Paradise Lost*, VI.625–26, the pun on "understand." "Had need from head to foot well understand / Not understood." Yale, 7:167

"I shall take occasion . . . to point out a beautiful passage of Milton evidently copied from a book of no greater authority, [than *The Destruction of Troy*] in describing the gates of hell. Book 2.v.879, he says,

> On a sudden open fly,
> With impetuous recoil and jarring sound,
> Th' infernal doors, and on their hinges grate
> Harsh thunder.

"In the history of *Don Bellianis*, when one of the knights approaches, as I remember, the castle of Brandezar, the gates are said to open 'grating harsh thunder upon their brasen hinges.'" Yale, 8:777

[J owned Milton's *Defensio pro Populo Anglicano*, his *Pro Se Defensio contra Alexandrum Morum*, and "Milton's Poems Vol. 2D." Reade, pp. 215 and 224.]

MONBODDO, JAMES, BURNETT, LORD*

"What strange narrowness of mind now is that, to think the things we have not known, are better than the things we have known." *Life*, 2:147

See also *Life*, 2:219, 259–60; 5:45–6, 77, 111, 242–43 for further jibes at him.

MORE, DR. HENRY*

J "did not much affect" him; he was "in Johnson's opinion, a visionary," one passage from whose writings J would "frequently cite" and "laugh at." *Life*, 2:162, n. 1

[And yet J may have owned More's works. Greene, p. 85.]

MORE, SIR THOMAS*

"it appears from *Ben Johnson* [*sic*], that his works were considered as models of pure and elegant style. The tale [quoted first] will

show what an attentive reader will, in perusing our old writers, often remark, that the familiar and colloquial part of our language, being diffused among many classes who have no ambition of refinement or affectation of novelty, has suffered very little change." *Hist. Eng. Lang. Dict.,* (G[2]ᵛ).
[J had More's works, 1557 (Greene, p. 85), and a copy of his *Utopia* (Reade, p. 214).]

MORER, THOMAS*

Short Account of Scotland . . .
"It is sad stuff, Sir, miserably written, as books in general then [1702] were." *Life,* 3:242–43 and 517

MUDGE, REV. ZACHARIAH*

"Notes upon the Psalms"
"he studied the sacred volumes in the original languages; with what diligence and success, his *Notes upon the Psalms* give sufficient evidence." *Life,* 4:77, quoted from the *London Chronicle* of May 2, 1769

Sermons
"'Mudge's Sermons' are good, but not practical. He grasps more sense than he can hold; he takes more corn than he can make into meal; he opens a wide prospect, but it is so distant, it is indistinct." *Life,* 4:98.
[J had both Mudge's Sermons and his Psalms. Greene, pp. 85–86.]

MULGRAVE, CONSTANTINE, JOHN PHIPPS, SECOND BARON*

Identified in *P.P.,* 10:179, as the man whose verses J would throw into his face.
[J owned "Phipps' voyage towards the north pole 1774." Greene, p. 91.]
See Poetry.

MUSIC*

"Of music Dr. Johnson used to say that it was the only sensual pleasure without vice." *J Misc.,* 2:[301]

"The delight which Music affords seems to be one of the first attainments of rational nature; wherever there is humanity, there is modulated sound. The mind set free from the resistless tyranny of painful want, employs its first leisure upon some savage melody." Dedication to Charles Burney's *Commemoration of Handel* (1785), Hazen pp. 32–33.

Dedication to the Queen of Dr. Charles Burney's *General History of Music* . . . (1796)
"The science of musical sounds, though it may have been depreciated, as appealing only to the ear, and affording nothing more than a momentary and fugitive delight, may be with justice considered as the art which unites corporal with intellectual pleasure, by a species of enjoyment which gratifies sense, without weakening reason; and which, therefore, the Great may cultivate without debasement, and the Good enjoy without depravation." Hazen, p. 29.

NEWTON, SIR ISAAC*

J is said to have remarked that "if Newton had flourished in ancient Greece, he would have been worshipped as a Divinity." *Life*, 2:125, n. 4

"no man knows as much Mathematicks as Newton." *Life*, 4:217

Had "Sir Isaac Newton applied to poetry, he would have made a very fine epick poem." *Life*, 5:35

NEWTON, BISHOP THOMAS*

Edition of *Paradise Lost*
"of which I had, however, so little use, that, as it would be injustice to censure, it would be flattery to commend it." Postscript to *Essay on Milton's Use and Imitation of the Moderns, Wks.*, 5:270

Dissertations on the Prophecies
"I fancy a considerable part of it was borrowed."; questions its greatness. *Life*, 4:285

NICHOLS, JOHN*

Anecdotes of William Bowyer
"I have looked often into your Anecdotes and you will hardly

thank a lover of literary history for telling you that he has been informed and gratified. *Letters,* 2:511

[J had Nichols's *Biographical and Literary Anecdotes of William Bowyer.* Greene, p. 87.]

NUGENT, DR. CHRISTOPHER*

Translation of *The Life of Benvenuto Cellini*
"Dr. Nugent seems to have carefully studied his author, and to have translated him with ease and freedom, as well as truth and fidelity." *Wks.* (1816), 2:197

OGDEN, DR. SAMUEL*

Sermons on Prayer
"I should like to read all that Ogden has written." *Life,* 3:248

OTWAY, THOMAS

Venice Preserved
Brutus, in *Julius Caesar,* says, "Swear priests, and cowards, and men cautelous." J comments, "This is imitated by Otway, 'When you bind me, is there need of oaths?'" Yale, 8:829

PARNELL, THOMAS

"the learning and genius of Parnell" *Life,* 3:155. *See* Biography.

PASSERATIUS

His "epitaph upon the heart of Henry, king of France, who was stabbed by Clement the monk" shows "how beautiful improprieties may become in the hands of a good writer."

Adsta, viator, et dolum regum vices.
Cor regis isto conditur sub marmore,
Qui jura Gallis, jura Sarmatis dedit;
Tectus cucullo hunc sustulit sicarius.
Abi, viator, et dolum regis vices.
Essay on Epitaphs, Wks., 5:263–64

[JEB has only "Epitaph by P. highly praised." *Wks.*, 9:442.]
[J quoted an English "translation of Passeratius's epitaph on Henry IV of France, published by Camden" for authority for Shakespeare's use of "Polack" in the first scene of *Hamlet.* Yale, 8:958.]

PATRICK, DR. SIMON*

J recommends his *Commentary upon the Historical Books of the Old Testament. Life,* 3:58

PENNANT, THOMAS*

Tour in Scotland
"Pennant has much in his notions that I do not like, but still I think him a very intelligent traveller." *Letters,* 2:247

"Books of Travels having been mentioned, Johnson praised Pennant very highly." *Life,* 3:271

"Pennant has greater variety of enquiry than almost any man, and has told us more than perhaps one in ten thousand could have done, in the time that he took. He has not said what he was to tell; so you cannot find fault with him, for what he has not told. If a man comes to look for fish, you cannot blame him if he does not attend to fowls." *Life,* 5:221

PERSIUS*

Satires I.27
"Persius has justly observed, that knowledge is nothing to him who is not known by others to possess it." *Adv.* 85, Yale, 2:413

PHILELPHUS*

"Next to the ancients, those writers deserve to be mentioned, who, at the restoration of literature, imitated their language and their style with so great success, or who laboured with so much industry to make them understood: such were *Philelphus* and *Politian, Scaliger* and *Buchanan,* and the poets of the age of *Leo the Tenth.*" *Harleian Library, Wks.,* 5:188

[Neither he nor Politian Angelus is accorded a separate entry in
JEB, although they, with George Buchanan and Joseph Scaliger,
are linked in *An Account of the Harleian Catalogue*. The passage
is quoted under "Renaissance 1" in JEB, p. 217, there being a
cross-reference to it under both Buchanan and Scaliger. One
·would not know J's opinion of either Politian or Philelphus
from JEB. Philelphus is almost surely Petrus Justinus Philelphus, editor of Caesar's *Commentaries* (1477).]

Philips, Ambrose

Epitome of Bishop Hacket's *Life of Archbishop Williams*
"free enough from affectation, but has little spirit or vigour . . ."
Lives, 3:314

Pococke, Richard*

Description of the East. See Twiss, Richard.

Poetry

Easy Poetry
"Easy poetry has been so long excluded by ambition of ornament,
and luxuriance of imagery, that its nature now seems to be
forgotten." *Idler* 77, Yale, 2:240

Bouts Rimés
Boswell mentioned "Miller of Batheaston's collection of verses by
fine people. Mr. Johnson said that *Bouts rimés* was a conceit, and
an old conceit *now.*" *P.P.*, 10:179

Boswell mentioned Captain Phipps. Johnson: "He was a blockhead for his pains. I should be able to throw Phipps's verses in
his face. Indeed *Bouts rimés* is a childish, a ridiculous thing."
P.P., 10:179. Cf. *Life*, 2:366–67, 517, and Mulgrave,
Constantine.

["Bouts Rimez (French). The last words or rhymes of a number of verses given to be filled up" (J's *Dict.*).]

POLITIAN, ANGELUS

See Philelphus.

POPE, ALEXANDER

Editor of Shakespeare (1725) quoted on Shakespeare's anachronisms
"These faults Pope has endeavored, with more zeal than judgment, to transfer to his imagined interpolators." *Pref. to S.,* Yale, 7:72

"Mr. Rowe and Mr. Pope were very ignorant of the ancient English literature." *Proposals,* Yale, 7:56

"Silence:" "composed . . . as early [as poem on "Solitude"], with much greater elegance of diction, musick of numbers, extent of observation, and force of thought . . ." Review of Joseph Warton's *Essay on the Writings and Genius of Pope, Wks.,* 6:41

Epistle to Mr. Jervas
The conclusion to the poem claimed "his highest admiration:"

> Led by some rule that guides, but not constrains,
> And finish'd more through happiness than pains.
> > *J Misc.,* 2:254

On the Countess of Burlington Cutting Paper
"those who aspire to gentle elegance, collect female phrases and fashionable barbarisms, and imagine that style to be easy which custom has made familiar . . ." J quotes the whole poem. *Idler* 77, Yale, 2:240–41.

Dunciad
Pope "wrote his 'Dunciad' for fame. . . . He delighted to vex them [the dunces], no doubt; but he had more delight in seeing how well he could vex them." *Life,* 2:334
[J had four volumes of Pope's works (Greene, p. 94), the transla-

tions of Homer, and "Pope's Misc[ellanies] 2 VOL." Reade, p. 226.]

Potter, Rev. Robert*

Potter's translation of Aeschylus
"I thought what I read of it *verbiage*." *Life,* 3:256

Priestley, Dr. Joseph*

"Speaking of Dr. Priestley (whose writings I saw he esteemed at a low rate), he said, 'You have proved him as different in *probity* as he is in learning.' I called him an 'Index-scholar;' but he was not willing to allow him a claim even to that merit. He said that 'he borrowed from those who had been borrowers themselves and did not know that the mistakes he adopted had been answered by others.'" *Lit. Anecd.,* 2:552

Prior, Matthew

To the Countess of Exeter, Playing on the Lute, ll. 19–20

> For nought but light itself, itself can show,
> And only kings can write, what kings can do.

"a pretty illustration . . ." *Ramb.* 143, Yale, 4:401

Quevedo y Villegas, Francisco Gomez de*

Visions
"One of the most striking passages in the visions of Quevedo, which stigmatises those as fools who complain that they failed of happiness by sudden death . . ." *Ramb.* 98, Yale, 4:49

Quintilian*

"To our language may be, under great justness, applied the observation of Quintilian, that speech was not formed by an analogy sent from heaven." *Plan of Eng. Dict., Wks.,* 5:11

[J had a number of editions of Quintilian's *de institutione oratoria.* Greene, p. 95]

RALEIGH, SIR WALTER

See Language.

RESTORATION WITS*

"The wits of Charles' time had seldom more than slight and superficial views, and their care was to hide their want of learning behind the colours of a gay imagination." *Idler* 69, Yale, 2:216

RICHARDSON, SAMUEL

Clarissa
He praised Richardson's "account of a House of bad fame." *P.P.,* 13:150

Mrs. Piozzi called Clarissa "a perfect character." "On the contrary (said he), you may observe there is always something she prefers to truth." Piozzi/Shaw p. 134
[J had "volumes of *Clarissa,* Eng. and Dutch." Greene, p. 97.]

ROBERT OF GLOUCESTER*

The author "writes apparently in the same measure with the foregoing author of St. *Margarite,* which polished into greater exactness, appeared to our ancestors so suitable to the genius of the *English* language, that it was continued in use almost to the middle of the seventeenth century." *Hist. Eng. Lang. Dict.,* (E[2]^r) *See also* Alexandrine.
[J had the two-volume edition of this work, edited by Thomas Hearne. Greene, p. 98.]

ROBERTSON, WILLIAM

History of America
"a sour book . . ." *P.P.,* 6:119

History of Charles V
"Dull." *P.P.*, 6:119
[J had three editions of the *History of America* and one of Robert-
son's *History of Scotland.* Greene, p. 98.]

ROUSSEAU, JEAN JACQUES

See Voltaire.

ROWE, NICHOLAS

Shakespeare "has speeches, perhaps sometimes scenes, which
have all the delicacy of Rowe, without his effeminacy." *Pref. to
S,* Yale, 7:91

Edition of Shakespeare (1709)
"The persons of the drama [*Twelfth Night*] were first enumerated,
with all the cant of the modern stage, by Mr. Rowe." Yale, 7:311
n. 1

King Philip in Shakespeare's *King John* says

>'Tis true fair daughter; and this blessed day
>Even in France shall be kept festival

J comments, "From this passage Rowe seems to have borrowed
the first lines of his *Fair Penitent.*"

>Altamont. Let this auspicious day be ever sacred,
>No mourning, no misfortunes happen on it
>Let it be marked for triumphs and rejoicings
>
>. . . . .
>
>This happy day that gives me my Calista.
>Yale, 7:416

[J was especially fond of this play, calling it "One of the most
pleasing tragedies on the stage." *Lives,* 2:67.]

[J had Rowe's translation of Claudius Quillet's *Callipaedia*. Reade, p. 227.]
See Pope, Alexander.

RUFFHEAD, OWEN*

Life of Pope
"He [J] censured Ruffhead's Life of Pope; and said, 'he knew nothing of Pope, and nothing of Poetry.'" *Life* 2:166–67

SANDERSON, BP. ROBERT*

See Barrow, Isaac.

SCALIGER, JULIUS CAESAR*

Scaliger "imitated" the "language and style" of the ancients "with so great success." *Harleian Library, Wks.,* 5:188

"I can scarcely conceive that if Scaliger had not considered himself as allied to Vergil by being born in the same country, he would have found his works so much superior to those of Homer." *Ramb.* 93, Yale, 4:132–33

[J had Scaliger's *De Causis Linguae Latinae* and his *Poetice.* Reade, pp. 217 and 229.]

SEED, JEREMIAH*

Sermons
"Seed has a very fine style; but he is not very theological." *Life,* 3:248

SEWARD, THOMAS*

"The ingenious editor of Beaumont and Fletcher . . ." Yale, 8:772

SHAKESPEARE, WILLIAM (GENERAL)

ANACHRONISMS

1. The Clown in *Twelfth Night* mentions "the bells of St. Bennet" and J notes: "When in this play he mentioned 'the bed of Ware,'

he recollected that the scene was in Ilyria, and added 'in England';
but his sense of the same impropriety could not restrain him from
the bells of St. Bennet." Yale, 7:324

2. Shakespeare "gives to all nations the customs of England,
and to all ages the manners of his own." Yale, 7:433

3. Jack Cade, in *2 Henry VI*, says "thou hast caused printing to
be used" and J objects, "Shakespeare is a little too early with this
accusation." Yale, 8:593

4. Caesar says "death, a necessary end, / Will come, when it will
come" and J comments: "This is a sentence derived from the
stoical doctrine of predestination, and is therefore improper in
the mouth of Caesar." Yale, 8:829

AUTHORSHIP

1. "But by the internal marks of a composition we may discover
the authour with probability though seldom with certainty."
Yale, 7:162

2. "That this play [*Two Gentlemen of Verona*] is rightly attributed
to Shakespeare, I have little doubt. If it be taken from him, to
whom shall it be given?" Yale, 7:173

3. "The three parts of *Henry VI* are suspected, by Mr. Theobald,
of being supposititious, and are declared, by Dr. Warburton, to
be 'certainly not Shakespeare's.' Mr. Theobald's suspicion arises
from some obsolete words; but the phraseology is like the rest of
our authour's stile, and single words, of which however I do not
observe more than two, can conclude little.

"Dr. Warburton gives no reason, but I suppose him to judge
upon deeper principles and more comprehensive views, and to
draw his opinion from the general effect and spirit of the composition, which he thinks inferior to the other historical plays.

"From mere inferiority nothing can be inferred; in the productions of wit there will be inequality. Sometimes judgment will err,
and sometimes the matter itself will defeat the artist. Of every
authour's works one will be the best, and one will be the worst.
The colours are not equally pleasing, nor the attitudes equally
graceful, in all the pictures of Titian or Reynolds.

"Dissimilitude of stile and heterogeneousness of sentiment, may
sufficiently show that a work does not really belong to the reputed
authour. But in these plays no such marks of spuriousness are
found. The diction, the versification, and the figures, are Shakespeare's. These plays, considered, without regard to characters
and incidents, merely as narratives in verse, are more happily

conceived and more accurately finished than those of *King John,
Richard II,* or the tragick scenes of *Henry IV.* and *V.* If we take
these plays from Shakespeare, to whom shall they be given? What
authour of that age had the same easiness of expression and flu-
ency of numbers?

"Having considered the evidence given by the plays themselves,
and found it in their favour, let us now enquire what corrobora-
tion can be gained from other testimony. They are ascribed to
Shakespeare by the first editors, whose attestation may be received
in questions of fact, however unskilfuly they superintended their
edition. They seem to be declared genuine by the voice of Shakespeare himself, who refers to the second play in his epilogue to
Henry V. and apparently connects the first act of *Richard III.* with
the last of the third part of *Henry VI.* If it be objected that the plays
were popular, and therefore he alluded to them as well known; it
may be answered, with equal probability, that the natural passions
of a poet would have disposed him to separate his own works
from those of an inferior hand. And indeed if an authour's own
testimony is to be overthrown by speculative criticism, no man can
be any longer secure of literary reputation." Yale, 8:611–12

4. An allusion to King Henry IV in the play *Richard II*
prompted J to comment that the "allusions to the plays of *Henry
VI.* are no weak proofs of the authenticity of these disputed
pieces." Yale, 8:625

5. "Though it is very difficult to decide whether short pieces
be genuine or spurious, yet I cannot restrain myself from express-
ing my suspicion that neither the prologue nor epilogue to this
play [*Henry VIII*] is the work of Shakespeare." Yale, 8:657

6. J, on *Titus Andronicus:* "That Shakespeare wrote any part,
though Theobald declares it incontestable, I see no reason for
believing." Yale, 8:750

CONCEITS

[*See* Yale, 7:198, 244, 272, 284, 370, 391, 412, 444; 8:553, 626,
714, 862, 876, 902.]

DECLAMATION

"Inactive declamation is very coldly heard, however musical or
elegant, passionate or sublime." Yale, 7:84. *See also* Yale, 7:197,
266.

DECORUM

See *Henry V,* Yale, 8:550; *2 Henry VI,* Yale, 8:592; and *Hamlet,* Yale, 8:982.

FAULTS

1. "Shakespeare is no great chronologer in his dramas." Yale, 7:146
2. "Nothing is more frequent among dramatick writers, than to shorten their dialogues for the stage." Yale, 7:432

IMAGERY

[*See* Yale, 7:193, 413, 482, 483; 8:541, 548, 564, 601, 604, 695, 707, 982. JEB (p. 131) only gives J's definition from his *Dictionary,* but no examples from Shakespeare.]

INVENTION

1. "Perhaps it would not be easy to find any authour, except Homer, who invented so much as Shakespeare." *Pref. to S.,* Yale, 7:90
2. "Success in works of invention is not always proportionate to labour." Yale, 7:452

LANGUAGE

1. "Shakespeare is the first considerable authour of sublime or familiar dialogue in our language." Yale, 7:52–3
2. "Shakespeare is very uncertain in his use of negatives." Yale, 7:297
3. "Shakespeare often confounds the active and passive adjectives." Yale, 7:314
4. "Our authour uses his verbal adjectives with great license." Yale, 7:367
5. Shakespeare's "elliptical diction" Yale, 7:382
6. "The particles in this authour seem often to have been printed by chance." Yale, 7:434
7. "Shakespeare often obscures his meaning by playing with sounds." Yale, 7:447
8. "Many expressions bordering on indecency or prophane-

ness are found in the first editions which are afterwards corrected." Yale, 7:469

9. "Concerning Shakespeare's particles there is no certainty." Yale, 7:477

10. "The licentiousness of our authour's diction" Yale, 7:484

11. "Our authour's licentious diction" Yale, 7:518

12. "Our authour's licentious English" Yale, 8:650

13. "The licentiousness of our authour forces us often upon far fetched [sic] expositions." Yale, 8:720

14. "The licentious and abrupt expressions of our authour" Yale, 8:874

15. "Neither genius nor practice will always supply a hasty writer with the most proper diction." Yale, 8:1003

METAPHORS

1. Broken. Yale, 8:981
2. Common. Yale, 8:844
3. Forced and unnatural. Yale, 8:774
4. Harsh. Yale, 7:177, 427, 481
5. Improper. Yale, 7:303
6. Incongruous. Yale, 8:733
7. Indelicate. Yale, 7:424
8. Mean. Yale, 8:527
9. Natural. Yale, 8:757
10. Not sublime. Yale, 8:652

[JEB, "*Metaphors*. Compare Similies," has seven examples of metaphor (p. 148) and "*Similies*. Compare Metaphors" (pp. 235–36) has five examples of similies without one of the twelve from Shakespeare.]

REVISION

1. "This play [*Richard II*] is one of those which Shakespeare has apparently revised; but as success in works of invention is not always proportionate to labour, it is not finished at last with the happy force of some of his other tragedies." Yale, 7:452

2. "An authour in revising his work, when his original ideas have faded from his mind, and new observations have produced new sentiments, easily introduces images which have been more

newly impressed upon him, without observing their want of congruity to the general texture of his original design." Yale, 8:1002

SIMILES

See Yale, 7:406, 479,; 8:580, 843, 999.

SHAKESPEARE, WILLIAM (THE PLAYS IN THE ORDER OF J'S 1765 SHAKESPEARE)

[J had the second folio, the second issue of the third folio and the editions of the plays by Warburton and Stockdale, as well as George Steevens's edition of twenty quartos and "12 volumes of Shakespeare's" (sic). Greene p. 103.]

THE TEMPEST

I.i.1   [Stage direction] Enter a Ship-master, and a Boatswain.
In this naval dialogue, perhaps the first example of sailor's language exhibited on the stage, there are, as I have been told by a skilful navigator, some inaccuracies and contradictory orders.
I.3

I.i.26   *Gonzalo.* I have great comfort from this fellow

It may be observed of Gonzalo, that, being the only good man that appears with the king, he is the only man that preserves his cheerfulness in the wreck, and his hope on the island.
I.4

I.i.57   *Gonzalo.* [A confused noise within.] Mercy on us!
We split, We split! Farwel, my wife and children!
Brother, farewel! we split, we split, we split!

As Gonzalo had no brother in the ship, this line should, I think, be given to Alonso the king, taking leave of his brother Sebastian, to which the next lines make the natural answer. Gonzalo had indeed no wife and children there, but that exclamation is the general cry in wrecks. Brother is useless, unless some brother had been afterwards mentioned.
All these lines have been hitherto given to Gonzalo, who has no

brother in the ship. It is probable that the lines succeeding the
"confused noise within" should be considered as spoken by no
determinate characters.

I.6

I.ii.28   *Prospero.* I have with such provision in mine art
                So safely order'd, that there is no soul,
                No, not so much perdition as an hair,
                Betid to any creature in the vessel

Thus the old editions read, but this is apparently defective. . . .
the authour probably wrote "no soil," no stain, no spot.

I.8

I.ii.155   *Prospero.* When I have deck'd the sea with drops full salt

To "deck" the sea, if explained, to honour, adorn, or dignify, is
indeed ridiculous, but the original import of the verb "deck" is,
"to cover;" so in some parts they say "deck the table:" This sense
may be borne, but perhaps the poet wrote "fleck'd," which I think
is still used in rustic language of drops falling upon water.

I.13

[J's *Dictionary:* "To deck. 1. To cover; to overspread. 3. To adorn;
to embellish."]

I.ii.218   *Ariel.* On their sustaining garments not a blemish

[*Steevens's note on this line introduces the emendation "sea-stained" from
Thomas Edwards's MSS.*]
This note of Mr. Edwards, with which I suppose no reader is
satisfied, shews with how much greater ease critical emendations
are destroyed than made, and how willingly every man would be
changing the text, if his imagination would furnish alterations.

1773:I.17

I.ii.250   *Prospero.*   Dost thou forget
                From what a torment I did free thee?

That the character and conduct of Prospero may be understood,
something must be known of the system of enchantment, which
supplied all the marvellous found in the romances of the middle ages.

I.17

I.ii.306 *Miranda.* The strangeness of your story put
Heaviness in me.

Why should a wonderful story produce sleep? I believe experience will prove that any violent agitation of the mind easily subsides in slumber, especially when, as in Prospero's relation, the last images are pleasing.

I.19

I.ii.321 *Caliban.* As wicked dew, as e'er my mother brush'd
With raven's feather from unwholsom fen,
Drop on you both!

His diction is indeed somewhat clouded by the gloominess of his temper and the malignity of his purpose; but let any other being entertain the same thoughts and he will find them easily issue in the same expressions.

I.20

I.ii.396 *Ariel.* Full fathom five thy father lies

Ariel's lays, however seasonable and efficacious, must be allowed to be of no great supernatural dignity or elegance, they express nothing great, nor reveal any thing above mortal discovery.

I.24–25

II.i.226 *Antonio.* For he's a spirit of persuasion, only
Professes to persuade the King, his son's alive.

Of this entangled sentence I can draw no sense from the present reading, and therefore imagine that the authour gave it thus:

For *he*, a spirit of persuasion, only
Professes to persuade.

I.38

II.i.259 *Antonio.* Keep in Tunis,
And let Sebastian wake.

There is in this passage a propriety lost which a slight alteration will restore.

Sleep in Tunis,
And let Sebastian awake.

I.39

II.i.277   *Antonio.* This ancient morsel, this Sir Prudence, who
                Should not upbraid our course.

For "morsel" Dr. Warburton reads "antient moral," very elegantly
and judiciously, yet I know not whether the authour might not
write "morsel," as we say a "piece of a man."

I.40

III.iii.47   *Gonzalo.*   which now we find,
                Each putter out of five for one will bring us
                Good warrant of.

This passage alluding to a forgotten custom is very obscure.

I.58

III.iii.86   *Prospero.*   so with good life,
                And observation strange, my meaner ministers
                Their several kinds have done.

This seems a corruption. I know not in what sense "life" can here
be used, unless for "alacrity, liveliness, vigour," and in this sense
the expression is harsh.

I.60

[The fourteenth definition of "life" in J's *Dictionary* is "Spirit;
briskness; vivacity; resolution."]

It is observed of *The Tempest* that its plan is regular; this the
Revisal thinks, what I think too, an accidental effect of the story,
not intended or regarded by the authour. But whatever might be
Shakespeare's intention in forming or adopting the plot, he has
made it instrumental to the production of many characters, diver-
sified with boundless invention, and preserved with profound skill
in nature, extensive knowledge of opinions, and accurate observation of life. In a single drama are here exhibited princes, courtiers,
and sailors, all speaking in their real characters. The operations
of magick, the tumults of a storm, the adventures of a desart
island, the native effusion of untaught affection, the punishment
of guilt, and the final happiness of the pair for whom our passions
and reason are equally interested.

1773:I.100

["It . . . authour" appeared first in the appendix to the 1765
edition.]

A MIDSUMMER NIGHT'S DREAM

I.i.47   *Theseus.* To leave the figure, or disfigure it.

[We should read, "To 'leve the figure," &c. i.e. "releve," to heighten or add to the beauty of the figure, which is said to be "imprinted by him." Warburton.]
I know not why so harsh a word should be admitted with so little need, a word that, spoken, could not be understood, and of which no example can be shown.

I.91

I.i.76   *Theseus.* But earthlier happy is the rose distill'd,

Thus all the copies, "yet earthlier" is so harsh a word, and "earthlier happy" for "happier earthly" a mode of speech so unusual, that I wonder none of the editors have proposed "earlier happy."

I.92

I.i.183   *Helena.* Your eyes are lode stars, and your tongue's sweet air
              More tuneable than lark to shepherd's ear

This was a compliment not unfrequent among the old poets.

1.97

I.i.202   *Hermia.* Take comfort; he no more shall see my face;
              Lysander and myself will fly this place.
              Before the time I did Lysander see,
              Seem'd Athens like a paradise to me.

Perhaps every reader may not discover the propriety of these lines. Hermia is willing to comfort Helena, and to avoid all appearance of triumph over her. She therefore bids her not to consider the power of pleasing, as an advantage to be much envied or much desired, since Hermia, whom she considers as possessing it in the supreme degree, has found no other effect of it than the loss of happiness.

I.98

I.ii   [Stage direction] Enter Quince, Snug, Bottom, Flute, Snowt, and Starveling.
In this scene Shakespeare takes advantage of his knowledge of the theatre, to ridicule the prejudices and competitions of the players. Bottom, who is generally acknowledged the principal actor, declares his inclination to be for a tyrant, for a part of fury, tumult, and noise, such as every young man pants to perform when he first steps upon the stage. The same Bottom, who seems bred in a tiring-room, has another histrionical passion. He is for

engrossing every part, and would exclude his inferiors from all possibility of distinction. He is therefore desirous to play Pyramus, Thisbe and the Lyon at the same time.

I.100

II.i.34 *Fairy.* Are you not he,
That fright the maidens of the villageree,
Skim milk, and sometimes labour in the quern,
And bootless make the breathless huswife chern

The sense of these lines is confused.

I.106

II.i.101 *Queen.* The human mortals want their winter here,
No night is now with hymn or carol blest

Titania's account of this calamity is not sufficiently consequential. "Men find no winter," therefore they sing no hymns, the moon provoked by this omission alters the seasons: That is, the alterations of the seasons produces the alteration of the seasons. I am far from supposing that Shakespeare might not sometimes think confusedly, and therefore am not sure that the passage is corrupted.

I.110

II.i.220 *Helena.* For that
It is not night when I do see your face

This passage is paraphrased from two lines of an ancient poet [Tibullus *Elegies,* IV.xiii.11–12],

Tu nocte vel atra
Lumen, et in solis tu mihi turba locis.

I.118

III.i. [Stage direction] Enter Quince, Snug, Bottom, Flute, Snout and Starveling.
In the time of Shakespeare there were many companies of players, sometimes five at a time, contending for the favour of the publick. Of these some were undoubtedly very unskilful and very poor, and it is probable that the design of this scene was to ridicule their ignorance, and the odd expedients to which they might be driven by the want of proper decorations. Bottom was perhaps

the head of a rival house, and is therefore honoured with an ass's head.

I.126

III.i.169 *Queen.* And for night-tapers crop their waxen thighs,
                And light them at the fiery glow-worm's eyes

I know not how Shakespeare, who commonly derived his knowledge of nature from his own observation, happened to place the glow-worm's light in his eyes, which is only in his tail.

I.132

III.ii.25 *Puck.* And, at our stamp, here o'er and o'er one falls

This seems to be a vicious reading. Fairies are never represented stamping, or of a size that should give force to a stamp.

I.134

IV.i. [Stage Direction] Continued, the Wood. Enter Queen of Fairies, Bottom, Fairies attending, and the King behind them.
I see no good reason why the fourth act should begin here when there seems no interruption of the action. In the old quartos of 1600 there is no division of acts, which seems to have been afterwards arbitrarily made in the first folio, and may therefore be altered at pleasure.

I.149

IV.i.103 *Theseus.* Go one of you, find out the forester,
                   For now our observation is perform'd
                   The honours due to the morning of May.

I know not why Shakespeare called this a *Midsummer-Night's Dream,* when he so carefully informs us that it happened on the night preceding May day.

I.153

[Edmond Malone's explanation satisfied most Shakespeareans. He imagined that the title "was suggested by the time it was first introduced on the stage, which was probably at Midsummer." *See* the 1821 *Shakespeare,* V.296.]

V.i.90 *Theseus.* Our sport shall be, to take what they mistake;
                And what poor duty cannot do,
                Noble respect take it in might, not merit.

The sense of this passage, as it now stands, if it has any sense, is this. "What the inability of duty cannot perform, regardful generosity receives as an act of ability though not of merit."

I.163

V.i.2–22 *Theseus.* More strange than true. I never may believe
These antick fables, nor these fairy toys

These beautiful lines are in all the old editions thrown out of metre.

I.160

V.i.391 *Oberon.* Through this house give glimmering light,
By the dead and drowsy fire

Milton perhaps had this picture in his thought.

Glowing embers through the room
Teach light to counterfeit a gloom. *Il Penseroso*

I.174

Of this play, wild and fantastical as it is, all the parts in their various modes are well written, and give the kind of pleasure which the authour designed. Fairies in his time were much in fashion; common tradition had made them familiar, and Spenser's poem had made them great.

I.176

TWO GENTLEMEN OF VERONA

[John Upton asked how "do painters distinguish copies from originals, and have not authours their peculiar style and manner from which a true critick can form as unerring a judgment as a painter?"]
A painter knows a copy from an original by rules somewhat resembling those by which criticks know a translation, which if it be literal, and literal it must be to resemble the copy of a picture, will be easily distinguished. Copies are known from originals even when the painter copies his own picture; so if an authour should literally translate his work he would lose the manner of the original. . . . But by the internal marks of a composition we may discover the authour with probability, though seldom with certainty.

I.179

I.i.70   [Stage direction] Enter Speed.

That this, like many other scenes, is mean and vulgar, will be universally allowed.

I.183

II.iii.21   *Launce.* I am the dog: no, the dog is himself, and I am the dog: oh, the dog is me, and I am myself

This passage is much confused, and of confusion the present reading makes no end. . . . I know not how much reason the authour intended to bestow on Launce's soliloquy.

I.201

II.iv.209   *Protheus.* 'Tis but her picture I have yet beheld,
And that hath dazeled my reason's light

This is evidently a slip of attention, for he had seen her in the last scene, and in high terms offered her his service.

I.210

II.v.24   *Speed.*   What an ass art thou? I understand thee not.
Launce.   What a block art thou, that thou canst not?
My staff understands me.

This equivocation, miserable as it is, has been admitted by Milton in his great poem. B. VI.ll.621, 623–27

> The terms we sent were terms of weight,
> Such as we may perceive, amaz'd them all
> And stagger'd many; who receives them right
> Had need from head to foot well *understand,*
> Not *understood,* this gift they have besides
> To shew us when our foes stand not upright.

I.211

II.vi.1   [Stage direction] Enter Protheus solus.

It is to be observed that in the first folio edition, the only edition of authority, there are no directions concerning the scenes. . . . I make this remark in this place, because I know not whether the following soliloquy of Protheus [II.vi.7ff] is so proper in the street.

I.213

II.vi.42   *Protheus.* Love, lend me wings to make my purpose swift,
As thou hast lent me wit to plot this drift!

I suspect that the authour concluded the act with this couplet, and that the next scene should begin the third act; but the change, as it will add nothing to the probability of the action, is of no great importance.

I.214

That this play is rightly attributed to Shakespeare, I have little doubt. If it be taken from him, to whom shall it be given? This question may be asked of all the disputed plays, except *Titus Andronicus*; and it will be found more credible, that Shakespeare might sometimes sink below his highest flights, than that any other should rise up to his lowest.

I.259

MEASURE FOR MEASURE

I.i.7   *Duke.* My strength can give you: then no more remains:
But that to your sufficiency, as your worth is able,
And let them work.

That the passage is more or less corrupt, I believe every reader will agree with the editors. I am not convinced that a line is lost, as Mr. Theobald conjectures, nor that the change of "but" to "put," which Dr. Warburton has admitted after some other editor, will amend the fault. There was probably some original obscurity in the expression, which gave occasion to mistake in repetition or transcription. I therefore suspect that the authour wrote thus,

Then no more remains
But that to your *sufficiencies* your worth is *abled*,
And let them work.

I.263

I.i.28   *Duke.* There is a kind of character in thy life,
That to th' observer doth thy history
Fully unfold

Either this introduction has more solemnity than meaning, or it has meaning which I cannot discover.

I.266

I.i.51   *Duke.* We have with a leaven'd and prepared choice
Proceeded to you

"Leaven'd choice" is one of Shakespeare's harsh metaphors.

I.268

I.ii.32   *1 Gentleman.* I had as lief be a list of an English kersey, as be pil'd, as thou art pil'd, for a French velvet.

The jest about the pile of a French velvet, alludes to the loss of hair in the French disease, a very frequent topick of our authour's jocularity.

I.270

I.ii.182   *Claudio.*   for in her youth
                    There is a prone and speechless dialect,
                    Such as moves men!

I can scarcely tell what signification to give to the word "prone." Its primitive and translated senses are well known. The authour may, by a "prone" dialect, mean a dialect which men are "prone" to regard, or a dialect natural and unforced as those actions seem to which we are "prone." Either of these interpretations is sufficiently strained; but such distortion of words is not uncommon to our authour.

I.276

I.iv.41   *Lucio.*   as blossoming time
                    That from the seedness the bare fallow brings
                    To teeming foyson, so her plenteous womb
                    Expresseth his full tilth and husbandry.

As the sentence now stands it is apparently ungrammatical, I read,

At blossoming time, &c.

That is, "as they that feed grow full, so her womb now at *blossoming time,* at that time through which the seed time proceeds to the harvest, *her womb shows what has been doing.*" Lucio ludicrously calls pregnancy "blossoming time," the time when fruit is promised, though not yet ripe.

I.281

II.i.173   *Escalus.* Which is the wiser here? Justice, or Iniquity?

These were, I suppose, two personages well known to the audience by their frequent appearance in the old moralities. The words therefore at that time produced a combination of ideas, which they have now lost.

I.289

II.ii.185   *Angelo.* Ever 'till this very Now,
                When men were fond, I smil'd and wonder'd how.

As a day must now intervene between this conference of Isabella with Angelo, and the next, the act might more properly end here, and here, in my opinion, it was ended by the poet.

I.301

II.iv.14   *Angelo.* Wrench awe from fools, and tie the wiser souls
                To thy false seeming?

Here Shakespeare judiciously distinguishes the different operations of high place upon different minds. Fools are frightened, and wise men are allured. Those who cannot judge but by the eye, are easily awed by splendour, those who consider men as well as conditions, are easily persuaded to love the appearance of virtue dignified with power.

I.304

II.iv.26   *Angelo.*   and even so
                The gen'ral subject to a well-wished king

"The gen'ral subjects to a well-wish'd king." So the later editions: but the old copies read "the *general subject* to a well-wish'd king." The "general subject" seems a harsh expression, but "general subjects" has no sense at all; and "general" was in our authour's time a word for "people," so that the "general" is the "people" or "multitude subject" to a king. So in *Hamlet,* "the play pleased not the *million,* 'twas caviare to the *general.*"

I.305

III.i.13   *Duke.* Thou art not noble;
                For all th' accommodations, that thou bear'st,
                Are nurs'd by baseness

Dr. Warburton is undoubtedly mistaken in supposing that by "baseness" is meant "self-love" here assigned as the motive of all human actions. Shakespeare meant only to observe, that a minute analysis of life at once destroys that splendour which dazzles the imagination. Whatever grandeur can display, or luxury enjoy, is procured by "baseness," by offices of which the mind shrinks from contemplation. All the delicacies of the table may be traced back to the shambles and the dunghill, and magnificence of building was hewn from the quarry, and all the pomp of ornaments, dug from among the damps and darkness of the mine.

I.313

III.i.17 *Duke.*   Thy best of rest is sleep,
          And that thou oft provok'st; yet grosly fear'st
          Thy death, which is no more.

I cannot without indignation find Shakespeare saying, that "death is only sleep," lengthening out his exhortation by a sentence which in the Friar is impious, in the reasoner is foolish, and in the poet trite and vulgar.

I.313

III.i.32 *Duke.* Thou hast nor youth, nor age;
          But as it were an after-dinner's sleep,
          Dreaming on both

This is exquisitely imagined. When we are young we busy our-selves in forming schemes for succeeding time, and miss the grati-fications that are before us; when we are old we amuse the languour of age with the recollection of youthful pleasures or performances; so that our life, of which no part is filled with the business of the present time, resembles our dreams after dinner, when the events of the morning are mingled with the designs of the evening.

I.314

III.i.37 *Duke.* Thou has neither heat, affection, limb, nor beauty
          To make thy riches pleasant.

[*Warburton asked, "But how does beauty make 'riches pleasant?'" and emended to "nor bounty"; i.e., "Thou hast neither the pleasure of enjoying riches thy self, for thou wantest vigour: nor of seeing it enjoyed by others, for thou wantest 'bounty.'"*]
I am inclined to believe that neither man nor woman will have much difficulty to tell how "beauty makes riches pleasant." Surely this emendation, though it is elegant and ingenious, is not such as that an opportunity of inserting it should be purchased by declaring ignorance of what every one knows, by confessing insen-sibility of what every one feels.

I.315

III.i.55   *Claudio.* Now, sister, what's the comfort?
           Isabella. Why, as all comforts are; most good in deed

If this reading be right, Isabella must mean that she brings something better than "words" of comfort, she brings an assurance of
"deeds." This is harsh and constrained.

I.317

III.i.114   *Claudio.* If it were damnable, he being so wise,
                        Why would he for the momentary trick
                        Be perdurably fin'd?

Shakespeare shows his knowledge of human nature in the conduct of Claudio. When Isabella first tells him of Angelo's proposal
he answers with honest indignation, agreeably to his settled principles, "thou shalt not do't." But the love of life being permitted
to operate, soon furnishes him with sophistical arguments, he
believes it cannot be very dangerous to the soul, since Angelo,
who is so wise, will venture it.

I.319

III.i.140   *Isabella.* Is't not a kind of incest, to take life
                         From thine own sister's shame?

In Isabella's declamation there is something harsh, and something
forced and far-fetched. But her indignation cannot be thought
violent when we consider her not only as a virgin but as a nun.

I.321

III.i.245   *Duke.*   only refer yourself to this advantage

This is scarcely to be reconciled with any established mode of
speech. We may read, "only *reserve yourself to*," or "only *reserve to*
yourself this advantage."

I.324

III.ii.38   *Duke.* That we were all, as some would seem to be,
                      Free from all faults, as faults from seeming free!

The interpretation of Dr. Warburton ["seeming" means "comeliness"] is destitute of authority; though "seemly" is "decent" or
"comely," I know not that "seeming" is ever used for "comeliness."
The sense is likewise trifling, and the expression harsh. To wish

"that men were as free from faults, as faults are free from comeliness" (instead of "void of comeliness") is a very poor conceit.

I.327

.III.ii.261 *Duke.* He, who the sword of heav'n will bear,
                    Should be as holy as severe:
                    Pattern in himself to know,
                    Grace to stand, and virtue go

To "pattern" is "to work after a pattern," and, perhaps, in Shakespeare's licentious diction, simply to "work."

I.335

IV.ii.61 *Claudio.* As fast lock'd up in sleep, as guiltless labour
                    When it lyes starkly in the traveller's bones.

Stifly. These two lines afford a very pleasing image.

I.344

IV.ii.87 *Duke.*   that spirit's possest with haste,
                    That wounds th' unresisting postern with these
                    strokes.

The line is irregular, and the "unresisting postern" so strange an expression, that want of measure, and want of sense might justly raise suspicion of an errour, yet none of the later editors seem to have supposed the place faulty except Sir Tho. Hanmer, who reads "th' unresting postern."

I.345

IV.ii.144 *Provost.*   fearless of what's past, present, or to come; insensible of mortality, and desperately mortal.

This expression is obscure. Sir Thomas Hanmer reads "mortally desperate." "Mortally" is in low conversation used in this sense, but I know not whether it was ever written.

I.348

[J's *Dictionary:* "Mortal, *adj.* 5. Extreme; violent. A low word."]

IV.iv.33 *Angelo.* Alack, when once our grace we have forgot,
                    Nothing goes right; we would, and we would not.

Here undoubtedly the act should end, and was ended by the poet; for here is properly a cessation of action, and a night intervenes, and the place is changed, between the passages of this scene and those of the next. The next act beginning with the following scene, proceeds without any interruption of time or change of place.

I.358

IV.v.1 [Stage direction) Enter Duke in his own habit, and Friar Peter.
        Duke. These letters at fit time deliver me.

Peter never delivers the letters, but tells his story without any credentials. The poet forgot the plot which he had formed.

I.358

IV.vi.3 *Isabella.*   yet I'm advis'd to do it,
            He says, to vail full purpose.

To interpret words with such laxity as to make "full" the same with "beneficial," [Warburton's explanation] is to put an end, at once, to all necessity of emendation, for any word may then stand in the place of another.

I.359

IV.vi.10 [Stage direction] Enter Peter.

This play has two Friars, either of whom might singly have served. I should therefore imagine that Friar Thomas, in the first act, might be changed, without any harm, to Friar Peter; for why should the Duke unnecessarily trust two in an affair which required only one. The name of Friar Thomas is never mentioned in the dialogue, and therefore seems arbitrarily placed at the head of the scene.

I.359

V.i.354 *Lucio.*   show your sheep-biting face, and be hang'd an hour:
            will't not off?

This is intended to be the common language of vulgar indignation.

I.374

V.i.446 *Isabella.* A due sincerity govern'd his deeds
            Till he did look on me

Angelo's crimes were such, as must sufficiently justify punishment, whether its end be to secure the innocent from wrong, or to deter guilt by example; and I believe every reader feels some indignation when he finds him spared. From what extenuation of his crime can Isabel, who yet supposes her brother dead, form any plea in his favour? "Since he was good 'till he looked on me, let him not die." I am afraid our varlet poet intended to inculcate, that women think ill of nothing that raises the credit of their beauty, and are ready, however virtuous, to pardon any act which they think incited by their own charms.

I.377

V.i.494 *Duke.* By this, lord Angelo perceives he's safe

It is somewhat strange, that Isabel is not made to express either gratitude, wonder or joy at the sight of her brother.

I.380

V.i.497 *Duke.* Look, that you love your wife; her worth, worth yours.

Sir T. Hanmer reads, "Her worth *works* yours. . . . The words are, as they are too frequently, an affected gingle, but the sense is plain. 'Her worth worth yours'; that is, her value is equal to your value; the match is not unworthy of you.

I.380

V.i.528 *Duke.* Thanks, good friend Escalus, for thy much goodness
I have always thought that there is great confusion in this concluding speech.

I.381

The time of the action is indefinite; some time, we know not how much, must have elapsed between the recess of the Duke and the imprisonment of Claudio; for he must have learned the story of Mariana in his disguise, or he delegated his power to a man already known to be corrupted.

I.382

[Compare Lennox: "How comes it to pass, that the Duke is so well acquainted with the Story of *Mariana,* to whom *Angelo* was betrothed, but abandoned by him on Account of the Loss of her Fortune?" (I.29–30). And *see* below pp. 97–98, 106, 118, 136, 145, 187, 191 for more similarities between J and Lennox.]

THE MERCHANT OF VENICE

I.ii.45 *Nerissa.* Then, there is the Count Palatine.

I am always inclined to believe, that Shakespeare has more allusions to particular facts and persons than his readers commonly suppose. The count here mentioned was, perhaps, Albertus a Lasco, a Polish Palatine.

I.393

I.11.74   *Nerissa.* How like you the young German, the Duke of Saxony's nephew?

In Shakespeare's time the Duke of Bavaria visited London, and was made Knight of the Garter.
  Perhaps in this enumeration of Portia's suitors, there may be some covert allusion to those of Queen Elizabeth.

I.395

II.i.24   *Morochius.* By this scimitar,
            That slew the Sophy and a Persian prince

Shakespeare seldom escapes well when he is entangled with geography. The Prince of Morocco must have travelled far to kill the Sophy of Persia.

I.404

II.ii.32   *Launcelot.* I will try conclusions with him.

So the old quarto. The first Folio, by a mere blunder, reads, try "confusions," which because it makes a kind of paltry jest, has been copied by all the editors.

I.406

II.vii.78   *Portia.* A gentle riddance—draw the curtains; go—
             Let all of his complexion chuse me so.

The old quarto edition of 1600 has no distribution of acts, but proceeds from the beginning to the end in an unbroken tenour. This play therefore having been probably divided without authority by the publishers of the first folio, lies open to a new regulation if any more commodious division can be proposed.

I.422

II.ix.70   *Arragon.* "Take what wife you will to bed"

Perhaps the poet had forgotten that he who missed Portia was never to marry any woman.

I.427

IV.i.29   *Duke.* Enough to press a royal merchant down

This epithet was in our poet's time more striking and better understood, because Gresham was then commonly dignified with the title of the "royal merchant."

I.452

[Sir Thomas Gresham, Lord Mayor of London, built the Royal exchange at his own expense.]

IV.i.90   *Shylock.* You have among you many a purchas'd slave,
              Which, like your asses, and your dogs, and mules,
              You use in abject and in slavish part,
              Because you bought them. Shall I say to you,
              Let them be free, marry them to your heirs?

This argument considered as used to the particular persons, seems conclusive. I see not how Venetians or Englishmen, while they practice the purchase and sale of slaves, can much enforce or demand the law of "doing to others as we would that they should do to us."

I.456

[J hated slavery. See *Life,* II.476–77 and III.200–204.]

IV.i.104   *Duke of Venice.* Upon my pow'r I may dismiss this court,
                Unless Bellario, a learned doctor,
                Whom I have sent for to determine this,
                Come here to day.

The doctor and court are here somewhat unskilfully brought together. That the Duke would, on such an occasion, consult a doctor of great reputation, is not unlikely, but how should this be foreknown by Portia?

I.456

V.i.32   *Lorenzo.* Who comes with her?
          Messenger. None, but a holy hermit, and her maid.

I do not perceive the use of this hermit, of whom nothing is seen or heard afterwards. The poet had first planned his fable some other way, and inadvertently, when he changed his scheme, retained something of the original design.

I.469

V.i.63   *Lorenzo.* Such harmony is in immortal souls!

>But whilst this muddy vesture of decay
>Doth grosly close us in, we cannot hear it.

[*Warburton: "sounds"*]
This passage is obscure. "Immortal sounds" is a harsh combination of words.

I.470

V.i.129   *Portia.* Let me give light, but let me not be light;
            For a light wife doth make a heavy husband

There is scarcely any word with which Shakespeare so much delights to trifle as with "light," in its various significations.

I.473

V.i.203   *Portia.* What man is there so much unreasonable,
            If you had pleas'd to have defended it
            With any terms of zeal, wanted the modesty
            To urge the thing held as a ceremony?

This is very licentiously expressed.

I.476

AS YOU LIKE IT

I.ii.28   *Celia.* Let us sit and mock the good housewife Fortune from
            her wheel

The wheel of fortune is not the "wheel" of a "housewife," Shakespeare has confounded fortune whose wheel only figures uncertainty and vicissitude, with the destinie that spins the thread of life, though indeed not with a wheel.

II.11

I.ii.121   *Le Bleu.* Three proper young men, of excellent growth and
            presence;—
            Rosalind. With bills on their necks: "Be it known unto all men
            by these presents"

Where meaning is so very thin, as in this vein of jocularity, it is hard to catch, and therefore I know not well what to determine; . . . I believe the whole conceit is in the poor resemblance of "presence" and "presents."

II.14

I.iii.29   *Rosalind.* The Duke my father lov'd his father dearly.
           Celia. Doth it therefore ensue, that you should love his son
           dearly? by this kind of chase, I should hate him

That is, by this way of "following" the argument. "Dear" is used
by Shakespeare in a double sense, for "beloved," and for "hurtful,
hated, baleful." Both senses are authorised, and both drawn from
etymology, but properly "beloved" is "dear," and "hateful" is
"dere." Rosalind used "dearly" in the good, and Celia in the bad
sense.
                                                                II.22

[J has only "To dere," meaning "To hurt. Obsolete" in his
Dictionary.]

II.iv.33   *Silvius.* O, thou didst then ne'er love so heartily.
           If thou remember'st not the slightest folly

I am inclined to believe that from this passage Suckling took the
hint of his song

    Honest lover, whosoever,
    If in all thy love there ever
  Were one wav'ring thought, thy flame
  Were not even, still the same.
    Know this
    Thou lov'st amiss,
    And to love true
  Thou must begin again and love anew, &c. [Sir John Suckling,
    Song]
                                                                II.33

II.iv.55   *Clown.*   as all is mortal in nature, so is all nature in love mor-
           tal in folly

In the middle counties, "mortal," from "mort" a great quantity,
is used as a particle of amplification; as, "mortal tall," "mortal
little." Of this sense I believe Shakespeare takes advantage to produce one of his darling equivocations.
                                                                II.34

II.vii.65   *Duke Senior.* For thou thyself hast been a libertine,
            As sensual as the brutish sting itself

Though the "brutish sting" is capable of a sense not inconvenient in this passage, yet as it is a harsh and unusual mode of speech, I should read the "brutish sty."

II.41

II.vii.94   *Orlando.* The thorny point
Of bare distress hath ta'en from me the shew
Of smooth civility

We might read "torn" with more elegance, but elegance alone will not justify alteration.

II.42

II.vii.167   *Duke Senior.* Set down your venerable burden

Is it not likely that Shakespeare had in his mind this line of the *Metamorphoses?* [XIII.624–25.]

*Patremque
Fert humerus, venerabile onus
Cythereius heros.*

II.45

III.ii.37   *Clown.* Truly, thou art damn'd, like an ill-rosted egg, all on one side.

Of this jest I do not fully comprehend the meaning.

II.50

III.ii.147   *Celia.* "Atalanta's better part"

Shakespeare was no despicable mythologist, yet he seems here to have mistaken some other character for that of Atalanta.

II.54

III.ii.196   *Rosalind.* One inch of delay more is a South-sea of discovery. I pr'ythee, tell me, who it is; quickly

[*Warburton:* "off discovery"]
This sentience is rightly noted by the commentator as nonsense, but not so happily restored to sense. . . . How much voyages to the South-sea, on which English had then first ventured, engaged the conversation of that time, may be easily imagined.

II.56

III.ii.417   *Rosalind.* I drave my suitor from his mad humour of love, to a living humour of madness

If this be the true reading we must by "living" understand "last-ing," or "permanent," but I cannot forbear to think that some antithesis was intended which is now lost; perhaps the passage stood thus, "I drove my suitor from a *dying* humour of love to a living humour of madness." Or rather thus, "from a mad humour of love to a *loving* humour of madness," that is, from a "madness" that was "love," to a "love" that was "madness." This seems some-what harsh and strained, but such modes of speech are not un-usual in our poet: and this harshness was probably the cause of the corruption.

II.63

[There is no adjectival definition of "living" in J's *Dictionary.*]

III.iii.17   *Clown.*   lovers are given to poetry; and what they swear in
                poetry, may be said, as lovers, they do feign

This sentence seems perplexed and inconsequent.

II.65

III.iv.7   *Rosalind.* His very hair is of the dissembling colour.
             Celia. Something browner than Judas's: marry his kisses are
                Judas's own children.
             Rosalind. I' faith, his hair is of a good colour.

There is much of nature in this petty perverseness of Rosalind; she finds fault in her lover, in hope to be contradicted, and when Celia in sportive malice too readily seconds her accusations, she contradicts herself, rather than suffer her favourite to want a vindication.

II.68

IV.i.165   *Orlando.* A man had a wife with such a wit, he might say, "Wit,
                whither wilt?"

This must be some allusion to a story well known at that time, though now perhaps irretrievable.

II.81

IV.iii.1   *Rosalind.* How say you now, is it not past two o'clock? I wonder
                much, Orlando is not here.

The foregoing noisy scene was introduced only to fill up an inter-val, which is to represent two hours. This contraction of time we might impute to poor Rosalind's impatience, but that a few minutes after we find Orlando sending his excuse. I do not see that by any probable division of the acts this absurdity can be obviated.

II.84

LOVE'S LABOUR'S LOST

I.i.75   *Biron.*   while truth the while
Doth falsly blind the eye-sight of his look

"Falsly" is here, and in many other places, the same as "dishonestly" or "treacherously." The whole sense of this gingling declamation is only this, that "a man by too close study may read himself blind," which might have been told with less obscurity in fewer words.

II.113

I.i.82   *Biron.*   Who dazzling so, that eye shall be his heed,
And give him light, that it was blinded by.

This is another passage unnecessarily obscure.

II.114

I.i.149   *Biron.*   Necessity will make us all forsworn
Three thousand times within this three years' space:
For every man with his affects is born:
Not by might master'd, but by special grace.

Biron amidst his extravagancies, speaks with great justness against the folly of vows. They are made without sufficient regard to the variations of life, and are therefore broken by some unforeseen necessity. They proceed commonly from a presumptuous confidence, and a false estimate of human power.

II.117

III.i.187   *Biron.*   And I to be a corporal of his file,
And wear his colours! like a tumbler's hoop!

The conceit seems to be very forced and remote, however it be understood.

II.147

IV.ii.1   [Stage Direction] Enter Dull, Holofernes, and Sir Nathaniel.

I am not of the learned commentator's [Warburton's] opinion that the satire of Shakespeare is so seldom personal. It is of the nature of personal invectives to be soon unintelligible; and the authour that gratifies private malice, *animam in volnere penit,* [Virgil, *Georgics* IV.138] destroys the future efficacy of his own writings, and sacrifices the esteem of succeeding times to the laughter of a day.

II.155

V.i.2 *Nathaniel.* Sir, your reasons at dinner have been sharp and sententious; pleasant without scurrility, witty without affectation, audacious without impudency, learned without opinion, and strange without heresy.

I know not well what degree of respect Shakespeare intends to obtain for this vicar, but he has here put into his mouth a finished representation of colloquial excellence. It is very difficult to add any thing to this character of the schoolmaster's table-talk, and perhaps all the precepts of Castiglione will scarcely be found to comprehend a rule for conversation so justly delineated, so widely dilated, and so nicely limited.

II.181

[Baldassarre Castiglione, *The Courtier*]

V.ii.69 *Princess.* None are so surely caught, when they are catch'd,
As wit turn'd fool; folly, in wisdom hatch'd
Hath wisdom's warrant, and the help of school;
And wit's own grace to grace a learned fool.

These are observations worthy of a man who has surveyed human nature with the closest attention.

II.189

V.ii.374 *Biron.* when we greet
With eyes best seeing heaven's fiery eye,
By light we lose light; your capacity
Is of that nature, as to your huge store
Wise things seem foolish, and rich things but poor.

This is a very lofty and elegant compliment.

II.203

V.ii.440 *Princess.* Your oath once broke, you force not to forswear.

"You force not" is the same with "you make no difficulty." This is a very just observation. The crime which has been once committed, is committed again with less reluctance.

II.205

V.ii.576   *Costard*   your lion, that holds a poll-ax sitting on a close-
            stool, will be given to A-jax

There is a conceit of "Ajax" and "a jakes."

II.211

THE WINTER'S TALE

I.ii.161   *Leontes.* Will you take eggs for mony?

This seems to be a proverbial expression, used when a man sees
himself wronged and makes no resistance.

II.242

[J was right; it is an early English proverb.]

I.ii.260   *Camillo.* Whereof the execution did cry out
            Against the non-performance

This is one of the expressions by which Shakespeare too frequently clouds his meaning. This sounding phrase means, I think,
no more than "a thing necessary to be done."

II.245

II.i.143   *Antigonus.* I would land-dam him

"Land-dam" is probably one of those words which caprice
brought into fashion and which, after a short time, reason and
grammar drove irrecoverably away.

II.259

III.i.1   *Cleomines.* The climate's delicate, the air most sweet,
           Fertile the isle.

[*Warburton pointed out that the temple of Apollo was not on an island,
and emended to "Fertile the soil."*]
Shakespeare is little careful of geography. There is no need of
this emendation in a play of which the whole plot depends upon
geographical errour, by which Bohemia is supposed to be a mari-
time country.

II.272

III.i.14   *Dion.* The time is worth the use on't.

[*Warburton:* use is . . . time on't]

Either reading may serve, but neither is very elegant.

II.273

III.ii.153   *Leontes.* Apollo, pardon
                My great prophaneness 'gainst thine Oracle!

This vehement retraction of Leontes, accompanied with the confession of more crimes than he was suspected of, is agreeable to
our daily experience of the vicissitudes of violent tempers, and
the eruptions of minds oppressed with guilt.

II.280

IV.i.4   *Time.* Impute it not a crime
                To me, or my swift passage, that I slide
                O'er sixteen years, and leave the growth untry'd
                Of that wide gap

[*Warburton:* gulf untry'd]
This emendation is plausible, but the common reading is consis-
tent enough with our authour's manner, who attends more to his
ideas than to his words.

II.288

IV.i.7   *Time.*   since it is in my power
                To o'erthrow law, and in one self-born hour
                To plant and o'erwhelm custom. Let me pass
                The same I am, ere ancient'st order was,
                Or what is now receiv'd.

The reasoning of Time is not very clear; he seems to mean, that
he who has broke so many laws may now break another; that he
who introduced every thing may introduce Perdita on her six-
teenth year; and he intreats that he may pass as of old, before any
"order" or succession of objects, ancient or modern, distinguished
his periods.

II.289

IV.i.30   *Time.* If ever you have spent time worse ere now:
                If never, yet that Time himself doth say,
                He wishes earnestly, you never may.

I believe this speech of Time rather begins the fourth act than
concludes the third.

II.290

IV.iv.21   *Perdita.*   How would he look, to see his work, so noble.
              Vilely bound up!

It is impossible for any man to rid his mind of his profession.
The authourship of Shakespeare has supplied him with a metaphor, which rather than he would lose it, he has put with no great
propriety into the mouth of a country maid. Thinking of his own
works his mind passed naturally to the binder. I am glad that he
has no hint at an editor.

II.298

IV.iv.120   *Perdita.*   violets dim,
                But sweeter than the lids of Juno's eyes

I suspect that our authour mistakes Juno for Pallas, who was the
"goddess of blue eyes."

II.302

IV.iv.742   *Clown.*   Advocate's the court-word for a pheasant

["This satire, on the bribery of courts, not unpleasant." Warbur-
ton] This satire or this pleasantry, I confess myself not well to
understand.

II.324

V.i.159   *Florizel.*   From thence; from him, whose daughter
               His tears proclaim'd his parting with her

This is very ungrammatical and obscure.

II.334

V.ii.99   *1 Gentleman.*   Who would be thence, that has the benefit of ac-
              cess? every wink of an eye, some new grace will be born: our
              absence makes us unthrifty to our knowledge.

It was, I suppose, only to spare his own labour that the poet put
this whole scene into narrative.

II.341

TWELFTH NIGHT

I.i.18   *Duke.*   O, when my eyes did see Olivia first,
              Methought, she purg'd the air of pestilence;
              That instant was I turn'd into a hart

This image evidently alludes to the story of Acteon, by which Shakespeare seems to think men cautioned against too great familiarity with forbidden beauty.

II.355

I.i.55 *Viola.* I'll serve this duke

Viola is an excellent schemer, never at a loss; if she cannot serve the lady, she will serve the Duke.

II.358

III.i.87 *Viola* My matter hath no voice, Lady, but to your own pregnant and vouchsafed ear.

"Pregnant" is a word in this writer of very lax signification. It may here mean 'liberal.'"

1773:IV.202

[The sixth and last definition of "pregnant" in J's *Dictionary* is "Free; kind. Obsolete." The passage above is quoted in exemplification.]

III.iv.166 *Sir Toby.* "Fare thee well, and God have mercy upon one of our souls: he may have mercy upon mine, but my hope is better, and so look to thyself."

It were much to be wished, that Shakespeare in this and some other passages, had not ventured so near profaneness.

II.417

IV.i.58 *Olivia.* He started one poor heart of mine in thee.

I know not whether here be not an ambiguity intended between "heart" and "hart."

II.426

V.i.18 *Clown.* so that, conclusions to be as kisses, if your four negatives make your two affirmatives, why, then the worst for my friends, and the better for my foes.

I do not discover much ratiocination in the Clown's discourse. . . . What the "four" negatives are I do not know.

II.434

[Both J (Yale, 8:326) and Lennox (I.249–50) comment on the

great humor of the comic characters and also agree on the want of credibility.]

THE MERRY WIVES OF WINDSOR

I.i.22   *Shallow.* The luce is the fresh fish, the salt-fish is an old coat.

I see no consequence in this answer. Perhaps we may read, "the salt-fish *is not* an old coat." That is, the "fresh-fish" is the coat of an ancient family, and the "salt-fish" is the coat of a merchant grown rich by trading over the sea.

II.452

I.i.203   *Simple.*   did you not lend it to Alice Shortcake upon Allhallowmas last, a fortnight afore Michaelmas?

[Theobald suggested that Shakespeare had written "'Martlemas' as the vulgar call it."]
This correction, thus seriously and wisely enforced, is received by Sir Tho. Hanmer, but probably Shakespeare intended a blunder.

II.459

II.i.4   *Mrs. Page.*   "tho' love use reason for his precisian, he admits him not for his counsellor"

Of this word [precisian], I do not see any meaning that is very apposite to the present intention.

II.472

[J's *Dictionary:* "Precisian. 1. One who limits or restrains. 2. One who is superstitiously rigorous."]

II.ii.60   *Mrs. Quickly.*   you have brought her into such a canaries

This is the name of a brisk light dance, and is therefore properly enough used in low language for any hurry or perturbation.

II.485

III.v.150   *Ford.*   if I have horns to make one mad, let the proverb go with me, I'll be horn-mad.

There is no image which our authour appears so fond of as that of a cuckold's horns. Scarcely a light character is introduced that does not endeavour to produce merriment by some allusion to horned husbands.

II.522

IV.i.1 [Stage direction] Enter Mrs. Page, Mrs. Quickly, and William.

This is a very trifling scene, of no use to the plot, and I should think of no great delight to the audience; but Shakespeare best knew what would please.

II.523

IV.ii.194 *Evans.* I spy a great peard under her muffler.

As the second stratagem, by which Falstaff escapes, is much the grosser of the two, I wish it had been practised first. It is very unlikely that Ford having been so deceived before, and knowing that he had been deceived, would suffer him to escape in so slight a disguise.

II.531

V.v.170 *Page.* Yet be cheerful, Knight; thou shall eat a posset to night at my house, where I will desire thee to laugh at my wife, that now laughs at thee.

The two plots are excellently connected, and the transition very artfully made in this speech.

II.554

This comedy is remarkable for the variety and number of the personages, who exhibit more characters appropriated and discriminated, than perhaps can be found in any other play.

Whether Shakespeare was the first that produced upon the English stage the effect of language distorted and depraved by provincial or foreign pronunciation, I cannot certainly decide. This mode of forming ridiculous characters can confer praise only on him, who originally discovered it, for it requires not much of either wit or judgment: its success must be derived almost wholly from the player, but its power in a skilful mouth, even he that despises it, is unable to resist.

The conduct of this drama is deficient; the action begins and ends often before the conclusion, and the different parts might change places without inconvenience; but its general power, that power by which all works of genius shall finally be tried, is such, that perhaps it never yet had reader or spectator, who did not think it too soon at an end.

1773:I.311

THE TAMING OF THE SHREW

I.i.9   *Lucentio.* A course of learning, and ingenious studies.

I rather think it was written "ingenuous studies," but of this and a thousand such observations there is little certainty.

III.15

IV.iii.55   *Petruchio.* With silken coats and caps, and golden rings,
                  With ruffs, and cuffs, and fardingals, and things.

Though "things" is a poor word, yet I have no better, and perhaps the authour had not another that would rhyme. I once thought to transpose the words "rings" and "things," but it would make little improvement.

III.73

IV.iii.193   [Stage direction] They bear off Sly.
                  Scene IX.
                  Before Baptista's House.

I cannot but think, that the direction about the tinker [inserted by Pope from *The Taming of A Shrew*], who is always introduced at the end of the acts, together with the change of the scene, and the proportion of each act to the rest, make it probable that the fifth act begins here.

III.78

THE COMEDY OF ERRORS

II.i.100   *Adriana.* But, too unruly deer, he breaks the pale
                  And feeds from home.

The ambiguity of "deer" and "dear" is borrowed, poor as it is, by Waller in his poem on the *Ladies Girdle.*

This was heav'n's extremest sphere,
The pale that held my lovely *deer.*

III.116

III.i.105   *Balthazar.* For slander lives upon succession

The line apparently wants two syllables: what they were cannot
now be known.

III.130

III.ii.64   *Antipholis of Syracuse.* My sole earth's heav'n, and my
heaven's claim.

When he calls the girl his "only heaven on earth," he utters the
common cant of lovers.

III.133

III.ii.122   *Antipholis of Syracuse.* Where France?
Dromio of Syracuse. In her forehead; arm'd and reverted,
making war against her hair.

Our authour, in my opinion, only sports with an allusion, in which
he takes too much delight, and means that his mistress had the
French disease.

III.135

IV.ii.39   *Dromio of Syracuse.* A hound that runs counter, and yet
draws dry-foot well;
One, that, before the judgment, carries
poor souls to hell.

For the congruity of this jest with the scene of action, let our
authour answer.

III.144

MUCH ADO ABOUT NOTHING

I.i.39   *Beatrice.* He set up his bills here in Messina, and challeng'd Cupid at the flight

The disuse of the bow makes this passage obscure.

III.175

I.i.183   *Benedick.*   or do you play the flouting Jack, to tell us Cupid
is a good hare-finder

I know not whether I conceive the jest here intended. . . . Perhaps the thought lies no deeper than this, "Do you mean to tell us as new what we all know already?"

III.180

I.i.240   *Benedick.* I will have a recheate winded in my forehead

That is, "I will wear a horn on my forehead which the huntsman may blow." A "recheate" is the sound by which dogs are called back. Shakespeare had no mercy upon the poor cuckold, his "horn" is an inexhaustible subject of merriment.

III.182

I.iii.13   *Don John.* I cannot hide what I am: I must be sad when I have cause, and smile at no man's jests; eat when I have stomach, and wait for no man's leisure

This is one of our authour's natural touches. An envious and unsocial mind, too proud to give pleasure, and too sullen to receive it, always endeavours to hide its malignity from the world and from itself, under the plainness of simple honesty, or the dignity of haughty independence.

III.186

II.i.365   *Don Pedro.*   to bring Signior Benedick and the Lady Beatrice into a mountain of affection the one with the other

"A mountain of affection with one another" is a strange expression, yet I know not well how to change it.

III.201

III.iv.53   *Beatrice.* By my troth, I am exceeding ill-hey ho!
            Margaret. For a hawk, a horse, or a husband?
            Beatrice. For the letter that begins them all, H.

This is a poor jest, somewhat obscured, and not worth the trouble of elucidation. Margaret asks Beatrice for what she cries, "hey ho;" Beatrice answers, for an "H," that is, for an "ache" or "pain."

III.229

IV.i.100   *Claudio.* O Hero! what a Hero hadst thou been

I am afraid here is intended a poor conceit upon the word "hero."

III.237

IV.i.249   *Leonato.* Being that I flow in grief,
            The smallest twine may lead me.

This is one of our authour's observations upon life. Men over-powered with distress eagerly listen to the first offers of relief, close with every scheme, and believe every promise. He that has no longer any confidence in himself, is glad to repose his trust in any other that will undertake to guide him.

III.243

ALL'S WELL THAT ENDS WELL

I.i.138   *Parolles*. He, that hangs himself, is a virgin

[Hanmer: "is like"] [Warburton: "As he . . . so is"]
I believe most readers will spare both the emendations, which I do not think worth a claim or a contest. The old reading is more spritely and equally just.

III.284

I.i.152   *Parolles*. Will you any thing with it?
          Helena. Not my virginity yet.

This whole speech is abrupt, unconnected and obscure.

III.285

I.ii.32   *King*. He had the wit, which I can well observe
           To day in our young lords: but they may jest,
           Till their own scorn return to them; unnoted
           Ere they can hide their levity in honour.

This is an excellent observation. Jocose follies, and slight offences, are only allowed by mankind in him that overpowers them by great qualities.

III.290

I.iii.92   *Clown*. That man should be at woman's command, and yet no hurt done!—tho' honesty be no puritan, yet it will do no hurt; it will wear the surplice of humility over the black gown of a big heart—I am going, forsooth.

Here is an allusion, violently enough forced in, to satirise the obstinacy with which the Puritans refused the use of the ecclesiastical habits, which was, at that time, one principal cause of the breach of union, and, perhaps, to insinuate, that the modest purity of the surplice was sometimes a cover for pride.

III.297

I.iii.165   *Helena.*   can't no other,
                    But I your daughter, he must be my brother?

The meaning is obscur'd by the elliptical diction.

III.300

II.i.141   *Helena.* When mir'cles have by th' greatest been deny'd.
                    Oft expectation fails, and most oft there

I do not see the import or connection of this line. As the next
line stands without a correspondent rhyme, I suspect that something has been lost.

III.311

II.iii.11   *Parolles.* So I say, both of Galen and Paracelsus.
                    Lafeu. Of all the learned and authentick fellows—
                    Parolles. Right, so I say.

As the whole merriment of this scene consists in the pretentions
of Parolles to knowledge and sentiments which he has not, I believe here are two passages in which the words and sense are
bestowed upon him by the copies, which the authour gave to
Lafeu.

III.318

II.iii.178   *King.* Smile upon this contract! whose ceremony
                    Shall seem expedient on the new-born brief,
                    And be perform'd to night

This, if it be at all intelligible, is at least obscure and inaccurate.

III.325

II.iii.233   *Lafeu.*   for doing, I am past; as I will by thee, in what mo-
                    tion age will give me leave.

The conceit which is so thin that it might well escape a hasty
reader, is in the word "past," "I am *past,* as I will be *past* by thee."

III.327

IV.iii.31   *1 Lord.*   I would gladly have him see his company anat-
                    omiz'd, that he might take a measure of his own judgment

This is a very just and moral reason. Bertram, by finding how
erroneously he has judged, will be less confident, and more easily
moved by admonition.

III.364

IV.iii.282 *Interpreter.* What's his brother, the other Captain Dumain?
             2 Lord. Why does he ask him of me?

This is nature. Every man is on such occasions more willing to
hear his neighbour's character than his own.

III.372

IV.v.8 *Countess.* I would, I had not known him!

This dialogue serves to connect the incidents of Parolles with the
main plan of the play.

III.377

V.i.34 *Helena.* I will come after you with what good speed
             Our means will make us means.

Shakespeare delights much in this kind of reduplication, sometimes so as to obscure his meaning.

III.381

V.ii.53 *Lafeu.*   tho' you are a fool and a knave, you shall eat

Parolles has many of the lineaments of Falstaff, and seems to be
the character which Shakespeare delighted to draw, a fellow that
had more wit than virtue.

III.384

V.iii.21 *King.* We're reconcil'd, and the first view shall kill
             All repetition

"The first interview shall put an end to all recollection of the
past." Shakespeare is now hastening to the end of the play, finds
his matter sufficient to fill up his remaining scenes, and therefore,
as on other such occasions, contracts his dialogue and precipitates
his action. Decency required that Bertram's double crime of cruelty and disobedience, joined likewise with some hypocrisy, should
raise more resentment; and that though his mother might easily
forgive him, his king should more pertinaciously vindicate his
own authority and Helen's merit: of all this Shakespeare could
not be ignorant, but Shakespeare wanted to conclude his play.

III.386

V.iii.65 *King.* Our own love, waking, cries to see what's done,
             While shameful hate sleeps out the afternoon.

These two lines I shall be glad to call "an interpolation of a player."
They are ill connected with the former, and not very clear or
proper in themselves.

III.388

V.iii.300   *Diana.*   He knows himself, my bed he hath defil'd,
                And at that time he got his wife with child;
                Dead tho' she be, she feels her young one kick:
                And there's my riddle; one, that's dead, is quick.
                And now behold the meaning.

This dialogue is too long, since the audience already knew the
whole transaction; nor is there any reason for puzzling the King
and playing with his passions; but it was much easier than to
make a pathetical interview between Helen and her husband, her
mother, and the King.

III.397

[Both J (Yale, 7:404) and Lennox (I.195) remark on the failure
of poetic justice, in that the ignoble Bertram is dismissed to
happiness.]

KING JOHN

I.i.24   *King John.*   Be thou as lightning in the eyes of France,
                For ere thou canst report, I will be there

The simile does not suit well: the lightning indeed appears before
the thunder is heard, but the lightning is destructive, and the
thunder innocent.

III.404

I.i.138   *Philip.*   Madam, and if my brother had my shape,
                And I had his, Sir Robert his, like him

This is obscure and ill expressed.

III.408

I.i.170   *Philip.*   Something about, a little from the right;
                In at the window, or else o'er the hatch,
              Who dares not stir by day, must walk by night,
                And have his have, however men do catch;
              Near or far off, well won is still well shot;
              And I am I, howe'er I was begot.

This speech, composed of allusive and proverbial sentences, is obscure.

III.411

[The second line above is proverbial as is the fourth, although the second should be "have is have."]

I.i.200   *Philip.* And so e'er answer knows what question would,
                    Saving in dialogue of compliment

[*Warburton:* Serving]
This passage is obscure; but such an irregularity, and perplexity runs thro' the whole speech, that I think this emendation not necessary.

III.412

I.i.225   *Philip.* Colbrand the giant

Colbrand was a Danish giant, whom Guy of Warwick discomfited in the presence of King Athelstan. The combat is very pompously described by Drayton in his *Polyolbion.*

III.413

II.i.183   *Constance.* I have but this to say,
                    That he's not only plagued for her sin,
                    But God hath made her sin and her plague
                    On this removed issue, plagu'd for her,
                    And with her. —Plague her sin; his injury,
                    Her injury, the beadle to her sin

This passage appears to me very obscure.

III.423

II.i.300   *French Herald.* Ye men of Angiers, open wide your gates
                    And let young Arthur Duke of Bretagne in;
                    Who by the hand of France this day hath
                        made
                    Much work for tears in many an English
                        mother,
                    Whose sons lye scatter'd on the bleeding
                        ground:
                    And many a widow's husband groveling lies,
                    Coldly embracing the discolour'd earth;
                    While victory with little loss doth play
                    Upon the dancing banners of the French,
                    Who are at hand triumphantly display'd,

> To enter conquerors, and to proclaim
> Arthur of Bretagne, England's King, and
> yours.

This speech is very poetical and smooth, and except the conceit of the "widow's husband" embracing "the earth," is just and beautiful.

III.427

II.i.312   *English Herald.* Rejoice, ye men of Angiers; ring your bells;
> King John, your King and England's, doth
> approach
> Commander of this hot malicious day.
> Their armours, that march'd hence so silver-
> bright,
> Hither return all gilt in Frenchmen's blood.
> There stuck no plume in any English crest,
> That is removed by a staff of France.
> Our colours do return in those same hands,
> That did display them, when we first
> march'd forth.

The English herald falls somewhat below his antagonist. "Silver armour gilt with blood," is a poor image.

III.428

II.i.325   *Citizen.* Heralds, from off our tow'rs we might behold,
> From first to last, the onset and retire
> Of both your armies, whose equality
> By our best eyes cannot be censured;
> Blood hath brought blood, and blows have answer'd
> blows;
> Strength match'd with strength, and power
> confronted, power.
> Both are alike, and both alike we like;
> One must prove greatest. While they weigh so even,
> We hold our town for neither; yet for both.

These three speeches seem to have been laboured. The citizen's is the best; yet "both alike we like," is a poor gingle.

III.428

II.i.455   *Philip.* Here's a stay.
> That shakes the rotten carcass of old death
> Out of his rags.

I cannot but think that every reader wishes for some other word in the place of "stay," which though it may signify an "hindrance," or "man" that "hinders," is yet very improper to introduce the next line. I read,

> Here's a *flaw,*
> That shakes the rotten carcass of old Death.

III.433

II.i.477   *Queen Elinor.* Lest zeal now melted by the windy breath
            Of soft petitions, pity and remorse,
            Cool and congeal again to what it was.

We have here a very unusual, and, I think, not very just image of "zeal," which in its highest degree is represented by others as a flame, but by Shakespeare as a frost.

III.434

III.i.68   *Constance.* I will instruct my sorrows to be proud;
            For Grief is proud, and makes his owner stout.
            To me, and to the state of my great grief,
            Let kings assemble

In *Much Ado About Nothing,* the father of Hero, depressed by her disgrace, declares himself so subdued by grief that "a thread may lead him." How is it that grief in Leonato and Lady Constance, produces effects directly opposite, and yet both agreeable to nature. Sorrow softens the mind while it is yet warmed by hope, but hardens it when it is congealed by despair. Distress, while there remains any prospect of relief, is weak and flexible, but when no succour remains, is fearless and stubborn; angry alike at those that injure, and at those that do not help; careless to please where nothing can be gained, and fearless to offend when there is nothing further to be dreaded. Such was this writer's knowledge of the passions.

III.440

III.i.102   *Constance.* You came in arms to spill my enemies blood,
             But now in arms, you strengthen it with yours.

I am afraid here is a clinch intended: "You came *in war* to destroy my enemies, but now you strengthen them *in embraces.*"

III.442

["Clinch" in J's *Dictionary:* "A word used in a double meaning; a pun; an ambiguity; a duplicity of meaning, with an identity of expression."]

III.i.133   *Philip.* And hang a calve's-skin on those recreant limbs.

Shakespeare, having familiarised the story to his own imagination, forgot that it was obscure to his audience; or, what is equally probable, the story was then so popular that a hint was sufficient at that time to bring it to mind, and these plays were written with very little care for the approbation of posterity.

III.443

III.i.47   *King John.* What earthly name to interrogatories
                    Can task the free breath of a sacred king?
                    Thou canst not, Cardinal, devise a name
                    So slight, unworthy, and ridiculous,
                    To charge me to an answer, as a Pope.

This must have been at the time when it was written, in our struggles with popery, a very captivating scene.

So many passages remain in which Shakespeare evidently takes his advantage of the facts then recent, and of the passions then in motion, that I cannot but suspect that time has obscured much of his art, and that many allusions yet remain undiscovered which perhaps may be gradually retrieved by succeeding commentators.

III.445

III.iv.61   *King Philip.* Bind up those tresses; O, what love I note
                    In the fair multitude of those her hairs;
                    Where but by chance a silver drop hath fall'n,
                    Ev'n to that drop ten thousand wiery friends
                    Do glew themselves in sociable grief;
                    Like true, inseparable, faithful loves,
                    Sticking together in calamity.

It was necessary that Constance should be interrupted, because a passion so violent cannot be borne long. I wish the following speeches had been equally happy; but they only serve to shew, how difficult it is to maintain the pathetick long.

III.459

III.iv.99   *Constance.*   had you such a loss as I,
                    I could give better comfort than you do.

This is a sentiment which great sorrow always dictates. Whoever cannot help himself casts his eyes on others for assistance, and often mistakes their inability for coldness.

III.460

IV.i.101   *Arthur.* Hubert, if you will, cut out my tongue,
                     So I may keep mine eyes.

This is according to nature. We imagine no evil so great as that which is near us.

III.467

IV.ii.79   *Salisbury.* His passion is so ripe, it needs must break.
            Pembroke. And when it breaks, I fear, will issue thence
                     The foul corruption of a sweet child's death.

This is but an indelicate metaphor, taken from an impostumated tumour.

III.471

IV.ii.231   *King John.* Hadst thou but shook thy head, or made a
                     pause,
                     When I spake darkly what I purposed:
                     Or turn'd an eye of doubt upon my face,
                     Or bid me tell my tale in express words;
                     Deep shame had struck me dumb, made me
                     break off,
                     And those thy fears might have wrought fears
                     in me.

There are many touches of nature in this conference of John with Hubert. . . . This account of the timidity of guilt is drawn *ab ipsis recessibus mentis,* from an intimate knowledge of mankind.

III.477

V.iv.11   *Melun.* Unthread the rude eye of rebellion

The metaphor is certainly harsh, but I do not think the passage corrupted.

III.495

There is extant another play of *King John,* published with Shakespeare's name, so different from this, and I think from all his other works, that there is reason to think his name was prefixed only to recommend it to sale. No man writes upon the same subject twice, without concurring in many places with himself.

III.503

RICHARD II

I.iii.19   *Mowbray.* Both to defend my loyalty and truth,
                 To God, my king and his succeeding issue

Such is the reading of the first folio; the later editions read "my" issue. Mowbray's "issue" was, by this accusation, in danger of an attainder, and therefore he might come among other reasons for their sake, but the old reading is more just and grammatical.

IV.13

I.iii.95   *Mowbray.* As gentle and as jocund, as to jest,
                 Go I to fight: truth hath a quiet breast.

[Warburton: to just]
The sense would perhaps have been better if the authour had written what his commentator substitutes, but the rhyme to which sense is too often enslaved, obliged Shakespeare to write "jest," and obliges us to read it.

IV.15

I.iii.206   *Mowbray.* Now no way can I stray,
                 Save back to England; all the world's my way.

Perhaps Milton had this in his mind when he wrote these lines.

> The world was all before them, where to chuse
> Their place of rest, and Providence their guide
>   [(*Paradise Lost*, XII:646–47).]

IV.20

I.iii.272   *Bolingbroke.*   and in the end
                 Having my freedom, boast of nothing else
                 But that I was a journeyman to grief?

I am afraid our authour in this place designed a very poor quibble, as "journey" signifies both "travel" and a "day's work."

IV.22

[In his *Dictionary* J derives "journey" from "*journee*, a day's work, Fr. and *man*."]

I.iii.308   *Bolingbroke.* Where-e'er I wander, boast of this I can,
                    Though banish'd; yet a true-born Englishman.

Here the first act ought to end, that between the first and second acts there may be time for John of Gaunt to accompany his son, return and fall sick. Then the first scene of the second act begins with a natural conversation, interrupted by a message from John of Gaunt, by which the king is called to visit him, which visit is paid in the following scene. As the play is now divided, more time passes between the two last scenes of the first act, than between the first act and the second.

IV.23

II.i.114   *Gaunt.* Thy state of law is bondslave to the law

This sentiment, whatever it is, is obscurely expressed.

IV.30

II.ii.38   *Queen.* 'Tis in reversion that I do possess;
                    But what it is, that is not yet known, what
                    I cannot name, 'tis nameless woe, I wot.

I am about to propose an interpretation which many will think harsh, and which I do not offer for certain. To "possess a man," is, in Shakespeare, to "inform him fully, to make him comprehend." To "be possessed," is, "to be fully informed." Of this sense the examples are numerous.

> I have *possest* him my most stay
> Can be but short. *Meas. for Meas.*
> Is he *possest* what sum you need. *Merch. of Venice*

I therefore imagine the Queen says thus:

> 'Tis in reversion—that I do possess.—

"The event is yet in futurity—*that I know with full conviction*—but what it is, that is not yet known." In any other interpretation she must say that "she possesses" what is not yet come, which, though it may be allowed to be poetical and figurative language, is yet, I think, less natural than my explanation.

IV.39

II.ii.62   *Queen.* So, Green, thou art the midwife of my woe,
                    And Bolingbroke my sorrow's dismal heir.

The authour seems to have used "heir" in an improper sense, an "heir" being one that "inherits by succession," is here put for one that "succeeds," though he "succeeds" but in order of time, not in order of descent.

IV.40

II.iv.1 [Stage direction] Enter Salisbury, and a Captain.

Here is a scene so unartfully and irregularly thrust into an improper place, that I cannot but suspect it accidentally transposed; which, when the scenes were written on single pages, might easily happen, in the wildness of Shakespeare's drama. This dialogue was, in the authour's draught, probably the second scene of the ensuing act, and there I would advise the reader to insert it, though I have not ventured on so bold a change. My conjecture is not so presumptuous as may be thought. The play was not, in Shakespeare's time, broken into acts; the two editions published before his death exhibited only a sequence of scenes from the beginning to the end, without any hint of a pause of action. In a drama so desultory and erratick, left in such a state, transpositions might easily be made.

IV.49

II.iv.8 *Captain.* The bay-trees in our country all are wither'd,
And meteors fright the fixed stars of heav'n;
The pale fac'd moon looks bloody on the earth;
And lean-look'd prophets whisper fearful change.
Rich men look sad, and ruffians dance and leap;
The one, in fear to lose what they enjoy;
Th' other, in hope t'enjoy by rage and war.
These signs forerun the death of kings—

This enumeration of prodigies is in the highest degree poetical and striking.

IV.49

III.ii.1 [Stage direction] Changes to the coast of Wales.

Here may be properly inserted the last scene of the second act.

IV.52

III.ii.26 *Carlisle.* Fear not, my Lord; that Pow'r, that made you king,
Hath pow'r to keep you king, in spight of all.
The means, that heaven yields, must be embrac'd

> And not neglected; else, if heaven would,
> And we would not heaven's offer, we refuse
> The profer'd means of succour and redress.

Of this speech the four last lines were restored from the first edition by Mr. Pope. They were, I suppose, omitted by the players only to shorten the scenes, for they are worthy of the authour and suitable to the personage.

IV.53

III.ii.93 *Richard.* Mine ear is open, and my heart prepar'd.
                       The worst is worldly loss thou canst unfold.

It seems to be the design of the poet to raise Richard to esteem in his fall, and consequently to interest the reader in his favour. He gives him only passive fortitude, the virtue of a confessor rather than a king. In his prosperity we saw him imperious and oppressive, but in his distress he is wise, patient, and pious.

IV.55

III.ii.154 *Richard.* Which serves as paste and cover to our bones.

A metaphor, not of the sublime kind, taken from a "pie."

IV.58

III.ii.207 *Richard.* By heav'n, I'll hate him everlastingly,
                        That bids me be of comfort any more.

This sentiment is drawn from nature. Nothing is more offensive to a mind convinced that his distress is without a remedy, and preparing to submit quietly to irresistible calamity, than these petty and conjectured comforts which unskilful officiousness thinks it virtue to administer.

IV.60

III.iii.156 *Richard.*   Where subjects' feet
                        May hourly trample on their sovereign's head;
                        For on my heart they tread now, whilst I live;
                        And bury'd once, why not upon my head?—

Shakespeare is very apt to deviate from the *pathetick* to the *ridiculous.* Had the speech of Richard ended at this line [156] it had exhibited the natural language of submissive misery, conforming its intention to the present fortune, and calmly ending its purposes in death.

IV.66

III.iv.26   *Gardiner.* Go, bind thou up yond dangling apricots

The conceit of rhyming "mocks" with "apricocks," which I hope
Shakespeare knew better how to spell . . .

IV.69

III.iv.100   *Queen.* Gard'ner, for telling me these news of woe,
            I would, the plants, thou graft'st, may never grow.

This execration of the queen is somewhat ludicrous, and unsuitable to her condition . . .

IV.72

IV.i.39   *Fitzwater.* And I will turn thy falshood to thy heart,
            Where it was forged, with my rapier's point.

Shakespeare deserts the manners of the age in which his drama
is placed very often, without necessity or advantage.

IV.74

[Richard II died in 1400; *OED* records a first use in 1553.]

IV.i.125   *Carlisle.* And shall the figure of God's majesty,
            His captain, steward, deputy elect,
            Anointed, crown'd, and planted many years,
            Be judg'd by subject and inferior breath,
            And he himself not present?

Here is another proof that our authour did not learn in King
James's court his elevated notions of the rights of kings. I know
not any flatterer of the Stuarts who has expressed this doctrine
in much stronger terms. It must be observed that the poet intends
from the beginning to the end to exhibit this bishop as brave,
pious, and venerable.

IV.77

IV.i.152   *Northumberland.* My lord of Westminster, be it your charge,
            To keep him safely till his day of tryal.

After this line, whatever follows, almost to the end of the act,
containing the whole process of dethroning and debasing King
Richard, was added after the first edition of 1598, and before the
second of 1615. Part of the addition is proper, and part might
have been forborn without much loss. The authour, I suppose,
intended to make a very moving scene.

IV.77

IV.1.181 *Richard.* Give me the crown. —Here, cousin, seize the
crown,
Here, on this side, my hand; on that side, thine.
Now is this golden crown like a deep well,
That owes two buckets, filling one another;
The emptier ever dancing in the air,
The other down, unseen and full of water;
That bucket down, and full of tears, am I;
Drinking my griefs, wilst you mount up on high.

This is a comparison not easily accommodated to the subject, nor
very naturally introduced. The best part is this line, in which he
makes the usurper the "empty" bucket.

IV.79

IV.i.322 *Carlisle.* The woe's to come; the children yet unborn
Shall feel this day as sharp to them as thorn.

This pathetick denunciation shews that Shakespeare intended to
impress his auditors with dislike of the deposal of Richard.

IV.83

V.i.46 *Richard.* For why? the senseless brands will sympathize
The heavy accent of thy moving tongue,
And in compassion weep the fire out;
And some will mourn in ashes, some coal-black,
For the deposing of a rightful king.

The poet should have ended this speech with the foregoing line
[45], and have spared his childish prattle about the fire.

IV.86

V.ii.56 *York.* What seal is that, which hangs without thy bosom?
Yea, look'st thou pale? let me see the writing.

Such harsh and defective lines as this, are probably corrupt, and
might be easily supplied, but that it would be dangerous to let
conjecture loose on such slight occasions.

IV.90

V.iii.5 *Bolingbroke.* Enquire at London, 'mong the taverns there:
For there, they say, he daily doth frequent,
With unrestrained loose companions.

This is a very proper introduction to the future character of Henry the Fifth, to his debaucheries in his youth, and his greatness in his manhood.

IV.92

V.iii.119   *York.* Speak it in French, King: say, "Pardonnez moy."

That is, "Excuse me," a phrase used when any thing is civilly denied. This whole passage is such as I could well wish away.

IV.97

V.v.51   *Richard.* My thoughts are minutes; and with sighs they jar,
          Their watches to mine eyes the outward watch;
          Whereto my finger, like a dial's point,
          Is pointing still, in cleansing them from tears.

I think this expression must be corrupt, but I know not well how to make it better.

IV.100

Jonson, who, in his *Catiline* and *Sejanus,* has inserted many speeches from the Roman historians, was, perhaps, induced to that practice by the example of Shakespeare, who had condescended sometimes to copy more ignoble writers. But Shakespeare had more of his own than Jonson, and, if he sometimes was willing to spare his labour, shewed by what he performed at other times, that his extracts were made by choice or idleness rather than necessity.

IV.105

[Both J (Yale 7:452) and Lennox (I.103) note that the Bishop of Carlisle's speech in the fourth act was copied from Holinshed.]

I HENRY IV

I.i.1   *King Henry.* So shaken as we are, so wan with care,
         Find we a time for frighted peace to pant,
         And breathe short-winded accents of new broils
         To be commenc'd in stronds a-far remote.

Shakespeare has apparently designed a regular connection of these dramatick histories from Richard the Second to Henry the Fifth. King Henry, at the end of *Richard the Second,* declares his purpose to visit the Holy Land, which he resumes in this speech.

The complaint made by King Henry in the last act of *Richard the Second,* of the wildness of his son, prepares the reader for the frolicks which are here to be recounted, and the characters which are now to be exhibited.

IV.109

I.i.5   *King Henry.* No more the thirsty entrance of this soil
Shall damp her lips with her own children's blood

That these lines are absurd is soon discovered, but how this non-sense will be made sense is not so easily told . . .

IV.110

I.i.9   *King Henry.* Those opposed eyes,
Which, like the meteors of a troubled heav'n,
All of one nature, of one substance bred,
Did lately meet in the intestine shock

[Warburton: opposed files]
This passage is not very accurate in the expression, but I think nothing can be changed.

IV.110

I.ii.208   *Prince Henry.* So, when this loose behaviour I throw off,
And pay the debt I never promised;
By how much better than my word I am,
By so much shall I falsifie men's hopes

This speech is very artfully introduced to keep the Prince from appearing vile in the opinion of the audience; it prepares them for his future reformation, and, what is yet more valuable, exhibits a natural picture of a great mind offering excuses to itself, and palliating those follies which it can neither justify nor forsake.

IV.123

I.iii.49   *Hotspur.* I, then all smarting with my wounds being cold

Whatever Percy might say of his "rage" and "toil," which is merely declamatory and apological, his wounds would at this time be certainly "cold," and when they were "cold" would "smart," and not before.

IV.126

I.iii.95   *Hotspur.*   to prove that true,

> Needs no more but one tongue; for all those
>   wounds,—
> Those mouthed wounds

This passage is of obscure construction.

IV.129

I.iii.103 *Hotspur.*   of swift Severn's flood;
> Who then affrighted with their bloody looks,
> Ran fearfully among the trembling reeds,
> And hid his crispe head in the hollow bank

This passage has been censured as sounding nonsense, which represents a stream of water as capable of fear. It is misunderstood. "Severn" is here not the "flood" but the tutelary power of the flood, who was frighted, and hid his head in "the hollow bank."

IV.129

I.iii.201 *Hotspur.* By heav'n, methinks, it were an easy leap,
> To pluck bright honour from the pale-fac'd moon

This sally of Hotspur may be, I think, soberly and rationally vindicated as the violent eruption of a mind inflated with ambition and fired with resentment; as the boastful clamour of a man able to do much, and eager to do more; as the hasty motion of turbulent desire; as the dark expression of indetermined thoughts.

IV.133

I.iii.286 *Worcester.* The King will always think him in our debt;
> And think, we deem ourselves unsatisfy'd,
> Til he hath found a time to pay us home.

This is a natural description of the state of mind between those that have conferred, and those that have received, obligations too great to be satisfied.

IV.137

II.iv.36 [Stage direction] Enter Francis the Drawer.

This scene, helped by the distraction of the drawer, and grimaces of the prince, may entertain upon the stage, but affords not much delight to the reader. The authour has judiciously made it short.

IV.152

II.iv.278 *Hostess.* Marry, my lord, there is a nobleman of the court

at door would speak with you; he says, he comes from
your father.
Prince Henry. Give him as much as will make him a royal man,
and send him back again to my mother.

I believe here is a kind of jest intended. He that had received a
"noble" was, in cant language, called a "nobleman": in this sense
the Prince catches the word, and bids the landlady "give him as
much as will make him a royal man," that is, a "real" or "royal"
man, and send him away.

IV.162

[A "noble" is defined in J's *Dictionary*, "2. A coin rated at six shil-
lings and eight pence; the sum of six and eight-pence". The second definition of "royal" is "State of a king".]

II.iv.345   *Prince Henry.* He that rides at high speed, and with a pistol
kills a sparrow flying.

Shakespeare never has any care to preserve the manners of the
time. "Pistols" were not known in the age of Henry.

IV.164

II.iv.369   *Prince Henry.* Thy state is taken for a joint-stool, thy golden
scepter for a leaden dagger, and thy precious rich crown
for a pitiful bald crown.

This answer might, I think, have better been omitted. It contains
only a repetition of Falstaff's mock-royalty.

IV.165

II.iv.398   *Falstaff.* Harry, I do not only marvel, where thou spendest
thy time, but also, how thou art accompany'd; for though
the camomile, the more it is trodden on, the faster it grows,
yet youth, the more it is wasted, the sooner it wears.

This whole speech is supremely comick.

IV.166

II.iv.500   *Prince Henry.* Go, hide thee behind the arras

The bulk of Falstaff made him not the fittest to be concealed
behind the hangings, but every poet sacrifices something to the
scenery; if Falstaff had not been hidden he could not have been
found asleep, nor had his pockets searched.

IV.170

II.iv.508   *Prince Henry.* This oily rascal is known as well as Paul's; go
            call him forth.
            Peto. Falstaff—fast asleep, behind the arras, and snorting like
            a horse.

The scenery here is somewhat perplexed.

IV.171

III.i.24   *Hotspur.* O, then the earth shook to see the heav'ns on fire,
           And not in fear of your nativity.

The poet has here taken, from the perverseness and contrarious-
ness of Hotspur's temper, an opportunity of raising his character,
by a very rational and philosophical confutation of superstitious
errour.

IV.173

["Philosophy" in J's *Dictionary* is defined as "1. Knowledge natural
or moral" and "4. The courses of sciences read in the schools." J
uses "philosophical" to mean according to natural science. *See also*
pp. 125, 158, 179, 185, 189.]

III.iii.26   *Falstaff.*   thou art the knight of the burning lamp.

This is a natural picture. Every man who feels in himself the pain
of deformity, however, like this merry knight, he may affect to
make sport with it among those whom it is his interest to please,
is ready to revenge any hint of contempt upon one whom he can
use with freedom.

IV.188

III.iii.112   *Falstaff.* There's no more faith in thee than in a stew'd
              prune; no more truth in thee than in a drawn fox

The propriety of these similies I am not sure that I fully
understand.

IV.191

III.iii.162   *Prince Henry.* And yet you will stand to it, you will not
              pocket up wrongs. Art thou not asham'd?

Some part of this merry dialogue seems to have been lost. I suppose Falstaff in pressing the robbery upon his hostess, had declared his resolution "not to pocket up wrongs or injuries," to
which the prince alludes.

IV.193

IV.i.61 *Worcester.* The quality and hair of our attempt
                     Brooks no division

The "hair" seems to be "the complexion, the character." The metaphor appears harsh to us, but, perhaps, was familiar in our authour's time.

IV.197

IV.i.97 *Vernon.* All furnisht, all in arms,
                   All plum'd like estridges, that with the wind
                   Baited like eagles, having lately bath'd

"To bait with the wind" appears to me an improper expression. . . . A more lively representation of young men ardent for enterprize perhaps no writer has ever given.

IV.198

IV.ii.19 *Falstaff.*   worse than a struck fowl, or a hurt wild duck.

The repitition of the same image disposed Sir Tho. Hanmer, and after him Dr. Warburton, to read, in opposition to all the copies, a struck "deer," which is indeed a proper expression, but not likely to have been corrupted.

IV.201

V.i.1 [Stage direction] The Camp at Shrewsbury.

It seems proper to be remarked, that in the editions printed while the authour lived, this play is not broken into acts. The division which was made by the players in the first folio seems commodious enough, but, being without authority, may be changed by any editor who thinks himself able to make a better.

IV.210

V.ii.59 *Vernon.* By still dispraising praise, valu'd with you.

[This foolish line is indeed in the Folio of 1623, but it is evidently the players' nonsense. Warburton]
This line is not only in the first folio, but in all the editions before it that I have seen. Why it should be censured as nonsense, I know not. To vilify praise, compared or "valued" with merit superior to praise, is no harsh expression. There is another objection to be made. Prince Henry, in his challenge of Percy, had indeed commended him, but with no such hyperboles as might represent

him above praise, and there seems to be no reason why Vernon should magnify the Prince's candour beyond the truth. Did then Shakespeare forget the foregoing scene? or are some lines lost from the Prince's speech?

IV.217

V.iv.107 *Prince Henry.* Death hath not struck so fair a deer to day
There is in these lines a very natural mixture of the serious and ludicrous produced by the view of Percy and Falstaff. I wish all play on words had been forborn.

IV.226

2 HENRY IV

These two plays [*1* and *2 Henry IV*] will appear to every reader, who shall peruse them without ambition of critical discoveries, to be so connected that the second is merely a sequel to the first; to be two only because they are too long to be one.

IV.235

Induction.1 *Rumour.* Open your ears; for which of you will stop
                     The vent of hearing, when loud Rumour
                     speaks?

This speech of Rumour is not inelegant or unpoetical, but is wholly useless, since we are told nothing which the first scene does not clearly and naturally discover. The only end of such prologues is to inform the audience of some facts previous to the action, of which they can have no knowledge from the persons of the drama.

IV.233

Induction.15 *Rumour.* Rumour is a pipe
                       Blown by surmises, jealousies, conjectures

Here the poet imagines himself describing Rumour, and forgets that Rumour is the speaker.

IV.233

I.i.157 *Northumberland.* But let one spirit of the first-born Cain
                          Reign in all bosoms, that each heart being
                          set
                          On bloody courses, the rude scene may end,
                          And darkness be the burier of the dead!

The conclusion of this noble speech is extremely striking. There is no need to suppose it exactly philosophical, "darkness" in poetry may be absence of eyes as well as privation of light.

IV.242

II.ii.89   *Page.* Marry, my lord, Althea dream'd, she was deliver'd of a firebrand; and therefore I call him her dream.

Shakespeare is here mistaken in his mythology, and has confounded Althea's firebrand with Hecuba's. The firebrand of Althea was real; but Hecuba, when she was big with Paris, dreamed that she was delivered of a firebrand that consumed the kingdom.

IV.267

II.ii.169   *Prince Henry.* How might we see Falstaff bestow himself to night in his true colours, and not ourselves be seen?
Poins. Put on two leather jerkins and aprons, and wait upon him at his table, as drawers.

This was a plot very unlikely to succeed where the Prince and the drawers were all known, but it produces merriment, which our authour found more useful than probability.

IV.269

II.iv.283   *Falstaff.* Ha! a bastard son of the King's! and art not thou Poins his brother?

The improbability of this scene is scarcely ballanced by the humour.

IV.283

III.i.106   *King Henry.* I will take your counsel;
And were these inward wars once out of hand,
We would, dear lords, unto the Holy Land.

This play, like the former, proceeds in one unbroken tenour through the first edition, and there is therefore no evidence that the division of the acts was made by the authour. Since then every editor has the same right to mark the intervals of action as the players, who made the present distribution. I should propose that this scene may be added to the foregoing act, and the remove from London to Gloucestershire be made in the intermediate time, but that it would shorten the next act too much, which has not even now its due proportion to the rest.

IV.291

IV.1.172   *York.* And present executions of our wills
             To us, and to our purposes, confin'd

This passage is so obscure that I know not what to make of it.

IV.310

IV.i.191   *Mowbray.* That, were our loyal faiths martyrs in love

In former editions:
        That, were our *royal* faiths martyrs in love.
If "royal faiths" can mean "faith in a king," it yet cannot mean it without much violence done to the language. I therefore read, with Sir T. Hanmer, "loyal" faiths, which is proper, natural, and suitable to the intention of the speaker.

IV.311

IV.ii.122   *Lancaster.* Some guard these traitors to the block of death,
             Treason's true bed and yielder up of breath.

It cannot but raise some indignation to find this horrible violation of faith passed over thus slightly by the poet, without any note of censure or detestation.

IV.317

IV.iii.87   *Falstaff.* Good faith, this same young sober-blooded boy doth
             not love me; nor a man cannot make him laugh

Falstaff speaks here like a veteran in life. The young prince did not love him, and he despaired to gain his affection, for he could not make him laugh. Men only become friends by community of pleasures. He who cannot be softened into gayety cannot easily be melted into kindness.

IV.323

IV.iv.47   *King Henry.*   it doth work as strong
             As aconitum, or rash gun-powder.

This representation of the Prince, is a natural picture of a young man whose passions are yet too strong for his virtues.

IV.323

IV.v.129   *King Henry.* England shall double gild his treble guilt

This line is indeed such as disgraces a few that precede and follow it.

IV.331

IV.v.146 *Prince Henry.* Let me no more from this obedience rise,
Which my most true and inward-duteous spirit
Teacheth this prostrate and exterior bending.

This is obscure in the construction, though the general meaning is clear enough. The order is, "this obedience which is taught this exterior bending by my duteous spirit"; or, "this obedience which teaches this exterior bending to my inwardly duteous spirit." I know not which is right.

IV.331

IV.v.219 *King Henry.* How I came by the crown, O God, forgive!
And grant it may with thee in true peace live.

This is a true picture of a mind divided between heaven and earth. He prays for the prosperity of guilt while he deprecates its punishment.

IV.334

V.v.63 *King Henry V.* Till then I banish thee, on pain of death,
As I have done the rest of my mis-leaders,
Not to come near our person by ten miles.

Mr. Rowe observes, that many readers lament to see Falstaff so hardly used by his old friend. But if it be considered that the fat knight has never uttered one sentiment of generosity, and with all his power of exciting mirth, has nothing in him that can be esteemed, no great pain will be suffered from the reflection that he is compelled to live honestly, and maintained by the king, with a promise of advancement when he shall deserve it.

I think the poet more blameable for Poins, who is always represented as joining some virtues with his vices, and is therefore treated by the Prince with apparent distinction, yet he does nothing in the time of action, and though after the bustle is over he is again a favourite, at last vanishes without notice. Shakespeare certainly lost him by heedlessness, in the multiplicity of his characters, the variety of his action, and his eagerness to end the play.

IV.353

I fancy every reader, when he ends this play, cries out with Desdemona, "O most lame and impotent conclusion!" . . .

Percy is a rugged soldier, cholerick, and quarrelsome, and has only the soldier's virtues, generosity and courage.

IV.355

HENRY V

I.Prologue.12   *Chorus.* or may we cram,
Within this wooden O

Nothing shews more evidently the power of custom over language, than that the frequent use of calling a circle an "O" could so much hide the meanness of the metaphor from Shakespeare, that he used it many times where he makes his most eager attempts at dignity and stile.

IV.361

I.Prologue.24   *Chorus.* Into a thousand parts divide one man,
And make an imaginary puissance.

This passage shews that Shakespeare was fully sensible of the absurdity of shewing battles on the theatre, which indeed is never done but tragedy becomes farce.

IV.362

I.i.38   *Canterbury.* Hear him but reason in divinity,
And, all admiring, with an inward wish
You would desire, the King were made a prelate.

The poet, if he had James in his thoughts, was no skilful encomiast; for the mention of Harry's skill in war, forced upon the remembrance of his audience the great deficiency of their present king; who yet with all his faults, and many faults he had, was such that Sir Robert Cotton says, "he would be content that England should never have a better, provided that it should never have a worse."

IV.365

I.i.86   *Canterbury.* The severals, and unhidden passages
Of his true titles

This line I suspect of corruption, though it may be fairly enough explained: the "passages" of his "titles" are the "lines" of "succession," by which his claims descend. "Unhidden" is "open, clear."

IV.367

I.ii.183   *Canterbury.* Therefore heaven doth divide
                          The state of man in diverse functions,
                          Setting endeavour in continual motion,
                          To which is fixed, as an aim or butt,
                          Obedience.

Neither the sense nor the construction of this passage is very obvious.

IV.375

II.Prologue.28   *Chorus.* And by their hands this grace of kings must
                            die,
                            If hell and treason hold their promises,
                            Ere he take ship for France; and in
                            Southampton.

I suppose every one that reads these lines looks about for a meaning which he cannot find. There is no connection of sense nor regularity of transition from one thought to the other. It may be suspected that some lines are lost, and in that case the sense is irretrievable.

IV.382

II.i.1   [Stage direction] Enter Corporal Nim, and Lieutenant Bardolph.

At this scene begins the connection of this play with the latter part of *King Henry IV*. The characters would be indistinct, and the incidents unintelligible, without the knowledge of what passed in the two foregoing plays.

IV.383

II.ii.126   *King Henry.* Oh, how hast thou with jealousy infected
                           The sweetness of affiance! Shew men dutiful?
                           Why so didst thou.

Shakespeare urges this aggravation of the guilt of treachery with great judgment. One of the worst consequences of breach of trust is the diminution of that confidence which makes the happiness of life, and the dissemination of suspicion, which is the poison of society.

IV.392

II.ii.165   *Grey.* My fault, but not my body, pardon, Sovereign.

This whole scene was much enlarged and improved after the first edition; the particular insertions it would be tedious to mention, and tedious without much use.

IV.394

II.iii.23   *Quickly.* I put my hand into the bed and felt them, and they were so cold as a stone; then I felt to his knees, and so upward, and upward, and all was as cold as any stone.

Such is the end of Falstaff, from whom Shakespeare had promised us in his epilogue to *Henry IV* that we should receive more entertainment. It happened to Shakespeare as to other writers, to have his imagination crowded with a tumultuary confusion of images, which, while they were yet unsorted and unexamined, seemed sufficient to furnish a long train of incidents, and a new variety of merriment, but which, when he was to produce them to view, shrunk suddenly from him, or could not be accommodated to his general design. That he once designed to have brought Falstaff on the scene again, we know from himself; but whether he could contrive no train of adventures suitable to his character, or could match him with no companions likely to quicken his humour, or could open no new vein of pleasantry, and was afraid to continue the same strain lest it should not find the same reception, he has here forever discarded him, and made haste to dispatch him, perhaps for the same reason for which Addison killed Sir Roger [*Spectator* 517], that no other hand might attempt to exhibit him.

IV.397

II.iv.105   *Exeter.*   upon your head
             Turning the widows' tears, the orphans' cries,
             The dead men's blood, the pining maidens' groans

The disposition of the images were more regular if we were to read thus:

                                  upon your head
             Turning the dead men's blood, the widow's tears
             The orphan's cries, the pining maidens' groans, &c.

IV.403

III.ii.138   *Fluellen.* Captain Macmorris, when there is more better opportunity to be requir'd, look you, I'll be so bold as to tell you, I know the disciplines of war; and there's an end.

It were to be wished that the poor merriment of this dialogue [ll.19–141] had not been purchased with so much profaneness.

IV.411

III.iii.30   *King Henry.* While yet the cool and temp'rate wind of grace
               O'er-blows the filthy and contagious clouds

This is a very harsh metaphor. To "over-blow" is to "drive away," or "to keep off."

IV.413

III.iv.1   [Stage direction] The French camp. Enter Catharine, and an old gentlewoman.

The scene is indeed mean enough, when it is read, but the grimaces of two French women, and the odd accent with which they uttered the English, made it divert upon the stage.

IV.414

III.v.50   *French King.* Rush on his host, as doth the melted snow
               Upon the vallies; whose low vassal seat
               The Alps doth spit and void his rheum upon.

The poet has here defeated himself by passing too soon from one image to another. To bid the French rush upon the English as the torrents formed from melted snow stream from the Alps, was at once vehement and proper, but its force is destroyed by the grossness of the thought in the next line.

IV.418

III.vi.99   *Fluellen.* The Duke hath lost never a man but one that is like to be executed for robbing a church, one Bardolph.

This is the last time that any sport can be made with the red face of Bardolph, which, to confess the truth, seems to have taken more hold on Shakespeare's imagination than on any other. The conception is very cold to the solitary reader, though it may be somewhat invigorated by the exhibition on the stage. This poet is always more careful about the present than the future, about his audience than his readers.

IV.423

III.vi.118   *Mountjoy.* Now, speak we on our cue,
                With voice imperial.

In our turn. This phrase the authour learned among players, and
has imparted it to kings.

IV.424

IV.i.176   *King Henry.* Every subject's duty is the King's but every subject's soul is his own.

This is a very just distinction, and the whole argument is well
followed, and properly concluded.

IV.439

IV.i.225   *King Henry.* Indeed, the French may lay twenty French
crowns to one, they will beat us, for they bear them on their
shoulders; but it is no English treason to cut French crowns,
and to morrow the King himself will be a clipper.

This conceit, rather too low for the King, has been already explained, as alluding to the venereal disease.

IV.441

IV.i.230–84   *King Henry.* Upon the King! let us our lives, our souls,
Our debts, our careful wives, our children
and
Our sins, lay on the King; he must bear
all.

There is something very striking and solemn in this soliloquy, into
which the King breaks immediately as soon as he is left alone.
Something like this, on less occasions, every breast has felt. Reflection and seriousness rush upon the mind upon the separation of
a gay company, and especially after forced and unwilling
merriment.

IV.441

IV.i.267   *King Henry.* Not all these, laid in bed majestical,
Can sleep so soundly as the wretched slave;
Who, with a body fill'd, and vacant mind,
Gets him to rest, cramm'd with distressful
bread,
Never sees horrid night, the child of hell,
But, like a lacquey, from the rise to set,
Sweats in the eye of Phoebus; and all night
Sleeps in Elysium

These lines are exquisitely pleasing. "To sweat in the eye of Phoebus," and "to sleep in Elysium," are expressions very poetical.

IV.443

IV.i.300   *King Henry.* Since that my patience comes after all,
                             Imploring pardon.

Shakespeare . . . certainly does not mean to represent the King as abandoned and reprobate.

IV.444

IV.iii.23   *King Henry.* God's will! I pray thee, wish not one man more.
                             By Jove, I am not covetous of gold.

The king prays like a Christian, and swears like a heathen.

IV.449

IV.iii.66   *King Henry.* And hold their manhoods cheap, while any
                             speaks,
                             That fought with us upon St. Crispian's day.

This speech, like many others of the declamatory kind, is too long. Had it been contracted to about half the number of lines, it might have gained force, and lost none of the sentiments.

IV.450

IV.iv.16   *French Soldier. Est-il impossible d'eschapper la force de ton bras?*
                Pistol. Brass, cur?
                             Thou damned and luxurious mountain goat,
                             Offer'st me brass?

[In the *Appendix* Hawkins urged that the pun on *bras* would be apparent only to a reader.]
If the pronunciation of the French language be not changed since Shakespeare's time, which is not unlikely, it may be suspected some other man wrote the French scenes.

1765 Appendix

IV.iv.46   *Fluellen.*   so also Harry Monmouth, being in his right wits
                             and his good judgments, turn'd away the fat Knight with
                             the great belly-doublet. He was full of jests and gypes, and
                             knaveries, and mocks; I have forgot his name.

This is the last time that Falstaff can make sport. The poet was loath to part with him, and has continued his memory as long as he could.

IV.460

IV.vii.63   *King Henry.* Besides, we'll cut the throats of those we have

The King is in a very bloody disposition. He has already cut the throats of his prisoners, and threatens now to cut them again. No haste of composition could produce such negligence; neither was this play, which is the second draught of the same design, written in haste.

IV.461

V.i.1   [Stage direction] The English Camp in France. Enter Fluellen and Gower.

This scene ought, in my opinion, to conclude the fourth act, and be placed before the last chorus.

IV.471

V.i.48   *Pistol.* I eat and eat I swear

Thus the first folio, for which the later editors have put, "I eat and swear." We should read, I suppose, in the frigid tumour of Pistol's dialect,

I eat and *eke* I swear.

IV.473

V.i.81   *Pistol.* News have I, that my Dol is dead i' th' spittle
            Of malady of France,
            And there my rendezvous is quite cut off

We must read, "my *Nell* is dead." Doll Tearsheet was so little the favourite of Pistol that he offered her in contempt to Nym. Nor would her death have "cut off his rendezvous"; that is, "deprived him of a home." Perhaps the poet forgot his plan.

IV.474

V.i.87   *Pistol.* To England will I steal, and there I'll steal;
            And patches will I get unto these cudgell'd scars,
            And swear, I got them in the Gallia Wars.

The comick scenes of Henry the Fourth and Fifth are now at an end, and all the comick personages are now dismissed. Falstaff and Mrs. Quickly are dead; Nym and Bardolph are hanged; Gadshill was lost immediately after the robbery; Poins and Peto have vanished since, one knows not how; and Pistol is now beaten into obscurity. I believe every reader regrets their departure.

IV.474

V.ii.1   *King Henry.* Peace to this meeting, wherefore we are met.
                  Peace, for which we are here met, be to this
                  meeting.

Here, after this chorus, the fifth act seems naturally to begin.

IV.475

V.ii.42   *Burgundy.* her hedges even pleach'd,
                  Like prisoners, wildly over-grown with hair.

This image of prisoners is oddly introduced. A "hedge even pleach'd" is more properly imprisoned than when it luxuriates in unpruned exuberance.

1773:VI.135

V.ii.121   *King Henry.* I'faith, Kate, my wooing is fit for thy understanding; I am glad thou canst speak no better English, for if thou couldst, thou wouldst find me such a plain king, that thou wouldst think I had sold my farm to buy my crown.

I know not why Shakespeare now gives the King such a character as he made him formerly ridicule in Percy. This military grossness and unskilfulness in all the softer arts, does not suit very well with the gaieties of his youth, with the general knowledge ascribed to him at his accession, or with the contemptuous message sent him by the Dauphin, who represents him as fitter for the ball room than the field, and tells him that he is not "to revel into dutchies," or win provinces "with a nimble galliard." The truth is, that the poet's matter failed him in the fifth act, and he was glad to fill it up with whatever he could get; and not even Shakespeare can write well without a proper subject. It is a vain endeavour for the most skilful hand to cultivate barrenness, or to paint upon vacuity.

IV.479

V.ii.291   *Burgundy.* Pardon the frankness of my mirth, if I answer you for that. If you would conjure in her, you must make a circle; if conjure up love in her in his true likeness, he must appear naked and blind. Can you blame her then, being a

> maid yet ros'd over with the virgin crimson of modesty, if
> she deny the appearance of a naked blind boy, in her naked
> seeing self? it were, my Lord, a hard condition for a maid
> to consign to.

We have here but a mean dialogue for princes; the merriment is
very gross, and the sentiments are very worthless.

IV.484

[Both J (Yale, 8:566) and Lennox (III.136–37) comment on the
poorness of the courtship scene between King Henry and Catharine of France.]

1 HENRY VI

II.v.2   *Mortimer.* Let dying Mortimer here rest himself.

I know not whether Milton did not take from this hint the lines
with which he opens his tragedy [*Samson Agonistes*].

IV.528

II.v.29   *Mortimer.* Just death, kind umpire of men's miseries.

That is, he that terminates or concludes misery. The expression
is harsh and forced.

IV.529

III.iii.78   *Burgundy.* These haughty words of hers
                    Have batter'd me like roaring cannon-shot

How these lines came hither I know not, there was nothing in the
speech of Joan haughty or violent, it was all soft entreaty and mild
expostulation.

IV.548

IV.v.16   *John Talbot.* The world will say, he is not Talbot's blood,
                      That basely fled, when noble Talbot stood.

For what reason this scene is written in rhyme I cannot guess. If
Shakespeare had not in other plays mingled his rhymes and blank
verses in the same manner, I should have suspected that this dialogue had been a part of some other poem which was never finished, and that being loath to throw his labour away, he inserted
it here.

IV.563

IV.vii.35   *Bastard.* How the young whelp of Talbot's raging brood
                    Did flesh his puny sword in Frenchmen's blood!

The return of rhyme where young Talbot is again mentioned, and in no other place, strengthens the suspicion that these verses were originally part of some other work, and were copied here only to save the trouble of composing new.

IV.568

V.iii.62   *Suffolk.* As plays the sunset upon the glassy streams,
                   Twinkling another counterfeited beam,
                   So seems this gorgeous beauty to mine eyes.

This comparison, made between things which seem sufficiently unlike, is intended to express the softness and delicacy of Lady Margaret's beauty, which delighted, but did not dazzle; which was bright, but gave no pain by its lustre.

IV.575

V.iv.89   *Joan La Pucelle.* But darkness and the gloomy shade of death
                        Inviron you, 'till mischief and despair
                        Drive you to break your necks, or hang
                        yourselves!

Perhaps Shakespeare intended to remark in this execration, the frequency of suicide among the English, which has been commonly imputed to the gloominess of their air.

IV.582

V.v.5   *King Henry.* And, like as rigour of tempestuous gusts
                    Provokes the mightiest hulk against the tide,
                    So am I driv'n by the breath of her renown,
                    Either to suffer shipwreck, or arrive
                    Where I may have fruition of her love.

This simile is somewhat obscure; he seems to mean, that as a ship is driven against the tide by the wind, so he is driven by love against the current of his interest.

IV.586

2 HENRY VI

It is apparent that this play begins where the former ends, and continues the series of transactions, of which it presupposes the

first part already known. This is a sufficient proof that the second
and third parts were not written without dependence on the first,
though they were printed as containing a complete period of
history.

V.3

I.i.121   *Warwick.* And are the cities, that I got with wounds,
                        Deliver'd up again with peaceful words?

The indignation of Warwick is natural, and I wish it had been
better expressed; there is a kind of jingle intended in "wounds"
and "words."

V.7

II.iii.30   *Queen Margaret.* God and King Henry govern England's
                                realm:
                                Give up your staff, Sir, and the King his
                                realm.

The word "realm" at the end of two lines together is displeasing;
and when it is considered that much of this scene is written in
rhyme, it will not appear improbable that the authour wrote, "govern England's *helm.*"

V.37

II.iv.67   *Gloucester.* Thy greatest help is quiet, gentle Nell

The poet has not endeavoured to raise much compassion for the
dutchess, who indeed suffers but what she had deserved.

V.43

II.iv.110   *Dame Eleanor.* Go, lead the way, I long to see my prison.

This impatience of a high spirit is very natural. It is not so dreadful to be imprisoned, as it is desirable in a state of disgrace to be
sheltered from the scorn of gazers.

V.44

III.i.210   *King Henry.* And as the butcher takes away the calf,
                            And binds the wretch, and beats it when it
                            strays

I am . . . inclined to believe that in this passage, as in many, there
is a confusion of ideas.

V.51

III.ii.160 *Warwick.* See, how the blood is settled in his face.

I cannot but stop a moment to observe that this horrible description is scarcely the work of any pen but Shakespeare's.

V.64

III.ii.333 *Suffolk.* You bid me ban, and will you bid me leave?

This inconsistency is very common in real life.

V.69

III.iii.32 *King Henry.* Close up his eyes, and draw the curtain close,
And let us all to meditation.

This is one of the scenes which have been applauded by the criticks, and which will continue to be admired when prejudice shall
cease, and bigotry give way to impartial examination. These are
beauties that rise out of nature and of truth; the superficial reader
cannot miss them, the profound can imagine nothing beyond
them.

V.73

IV.i.1 *Captain Whitmore.* The gaudy, babbling, and remorseful day
Is crept into the bosom of the sea

The epithet "babbling" applied to day by a man about to commit
murder, is exquisitely beautiful. Guilt afraid of light, considers
darkness as a natural shelter, and makes night the confidante of
those actions which cannot be trusted to the "tell-tale day."

V.74

IV.i.70 *Captain Whitmore.* Poole? Sir Poole? Lord?
Ay, kennel—puddle—sink

The dissonance of this broken line makes it almost certain that
we should read with a kind of ludicrous climax,

Poole? *Sir* Poole? *Lord* Poole?

He then plays upon the name, "Poole, kennel, puddle."

V.76

IV.i.135 *Suffolk.* A Roman sworder and banditto slave
Murder'd sweet Tully; Brutus' bastard hand

Stabb'd Julius Caesar; savage islanders
Pompey the Great

The poet seems to have confounded the story of Pompey with some other.

V.78

IV.ii.332 *Jack Cade.* For our enemies shall fall before us.

He alludes to his name "Cade," from *cado,* Lat. "to fall." He has too much learning for his character.

V.80

IV.vii.49 *Jack Cade.* Marry, thou ought'st not to let thy horse wear a cloak when honester men than thou go in their hose and doublets.

This is a reproach truly characteristical. Nothing gives so much offence to the lower ranks of mankind as the sight of superfluities merely ostentatious.

V.91

IV.x.77 *Alexander Iden.* Die damned wretch, the curse of her that bare thee

Not to dwell upon the wickedness of this horrid wish, with which Iden debases his character, this whole speech is wild and confused.

V.101

3 HENRY VI

I.i.1 *Warwick.* I wonder, how the King escap'd our hands!

This play is only divided from the former for the convenience of exhibition; for the series of action is continued without interruption, nor are any two scenes of any play more closely connected than the first scene of this play with the last of the former.

V.119

II.i.48 *Edward.* Oh, speak no more! for I have heard too much.
Richard. Say, how he dy'd, for I will hear it all.

The generous tenderness of Edward, and savage fortitude of

Richard, are well distinguished by their different reception of their father's death.

V.142

II.i.130   *Warwick.* Our soldiers, like the night-owl's lazy flight,
                        Or like a lazy thresher with a flail,
                        Fell gently down

This image is not very congruous to the subject, nor was it necessary to the comparison, which is happily enough compleated by the thresher.

V.144

II.v.21   *King Henry.* O God! Methinks it were a happy life
                          To be no better than a homely swain

This speech is mournful and soft, exquisitely suited to the character of the King, and makes a pleasing interchange, by affording, amidst the tumult and horrour of the battle, an unexpected glimpse of rural innocence and pastoral tranquility.

V.156

II.v.77   *King Henry.* And let our hearts and eyes, like civil war,
                          Be blind with tears, and break o'er-charg'd with
                          grief.

The meaning is here inaccurately expressed. The King intends to say that the state of their "hearts and eyes" shall be like that of the kingdom in a "civil war," all shall be destroyed by power formed within themselves.

V.158

III.i.16   *King Henry.* Thy place is fill'd, thy scepter wrung from thee;
                           Thy balm washt off, wherewith thou wast
                           anointed

It is an image very frequent in the works of Shakespeare. So again in this scene,

I was anointed King.

It is common in these plays to find the same images, whether jocular or serious, frequently recurring.

V.165

III.i.16   *King Henry.* Widow, we will consider of our suit,
　　　　　　　　And come some other time to know your mind.

This is a very lively and spritely dialogue; the reciprocation is quicker than is common in Shakespeare.

V.168

II.ii.165   *Gloucester.* Then since this earth affords no joy to me,
　　　　　　　　But to command, to check, to o'er-bear such
　　　　　　　　As are of better person than myself;
　　　　　　　　I'll make my heav'n to dream upon the crown

Richard speaks here the language of nature. Whoever is stigmatized with deformity has a constant source of envy in his mind, and would counterballance by some other superiority these advantages which he feels himself to want.

V.173

III.iii.154   *Warwick.* You have a father able to maintain you

This seems ironical. The poverty of Margaret's father is a very frequent topick of reproach.

V.180

IV.viii.1   *Earl of Warwick.* What counsel, Lords? Edward from Belgia,
　　　　　　　　With hasty Germans, and blunt Hollanders,
　　　　　　　　Hath pass'd in safety through the narrow
　　　　　　　　seas;
　　　　　　　　And with his troops doth march amain to
　　　　　　　　London;
　　　　　　　　And many giddy people flock to him.
　　　King Henry. Let's levy men, and beat him back again.

This line expresses a spirit of war so unsuitable to the character of Henry, that I would give the first cold speech to the King, and the brisk answer to Warwick.

V.203

V.iv.67   [Stage direction.] March. Enter King Edward, Gloucester, Clarence, and soldiers, on the other side of the stage.

This scene is ill-contrived, in which the King and Queen appear at once on the stage at the head of opposite armies. It had been easy to make one retire before the other entered.

V.215

V.v.65   *Queen Margaret.* But if you ever chance to have a child,
                        Look in his youth to have him so cut off;
                        As, deathsmen! you have rid this sweet
                        young prince.

The condition of this warlike queen would move compassion could it be forgotten that she gave York, to wipe his eyes in his captivity, a handkerchief stained with his young child's blood.

V.218

RICHARD III

I.i.2   *Gloucester.* He capers nimbly in a lady's chamber

War "capers." This is poetical, though a little harsh; if it be York that capers, the antecedent is at such a distance that it is almost forgotten.

V.230

I.i.19   *Gloucester.* Cheated of feature by dissembling nature

"Dissembling" is here put very licentiously for "fraudful, deceitful."

V.230

I.i.28   *Gloucester.* And therefore, since I cannot prove a lover,
                        To entertain these fair well-spoken days,
                        I am determined to prove a villain

Shakespeare very diligently inculcates, that the wickedness of Richard proceeded from his deformity, from the envy that rose at the comparison of his own person with others, and which incited him to disturb the pleasures that he could not partake.

V.230

I.i.108   *Gloucester.* And whatsoe'er you will employ me in,
                        Were it to call King Edward's widow sister,
                        I will perform it to infranchise you.

This is a very covert and subtle manner of insinuating treason.

V.233

II.i.103   *King Edward.* Have I a tongue to doom my brother's death?

This lamentation is very tender and pathetick. The recollection of the good qualities of the dead is very natural, and no less naturally does the King endeavour to communicate the crime to others.

V.269

II.ii.69   *Queen Elizabeth.* That I, being govern'd by the wat'ry moon,
May send forth plenteous tears to drown the world.

That I may live hereafter under the influence of the moon, which governs the tides, and, by the help of that influence, drown the world. The introduction of the moon is not very natural.

V.272

III.vii.246   *Gloucester.* [To the Clergymen.]
Come let us to our holy work again.
—Farewel, my cousin; farewel gentle friends.

To this act should, perhaps, be added the next scene, so will the coronation pass between the acts; and there will not only be a proper interval of action, but the conclusion will be more forcible.

V.312

IV.i.101   *Queen Elizabeth.* Rude ragged nurse! old sullen playfellow

To call the Tower "nurse" and "playfellow" is very harsh: perhaps part of this speech is addressed to the Tower, and part to the Lieutenant.

V.316

IV.i.102   *Queen Elizabeth.* use my babies well!
So foolish sorrow bids your stones farewel.

Hither the third act should be extended, and here it very properly ends with a pause of action.

V.316

IV.iv.15   *Queen Margaret.* Hover about her; say that right for right
Hath dimm'd your infant-morn to aged night.

This is one of those conceits which our authour may be suspected of loving better than propriety.

V.323

IV.iv.199 *King Richard.* Stay, Madam, I must speak a word with you.

On this dialogue 'tis not necessary to bestow much criticism: part of it is ridiculous, and the whole improbable.

V.329

V.i.28 *Buckingham.* Come, Sirs, convey me to the block of shame; Wrong hath but wrong, and blame the due of blame.

This scene should, in my opinion, be added to the foregoing act, so the fourth act will have a more full and striking conclusion, and the fifth act will comprise the business of the important day, which put an end to the competition of York and Lancaster.

V.343

V.iii.177 *King Richard.* Give me another horse—bind up my wounds— Have mercy, Jesu—soft, I did but dream.

There is in this, as in many of our authour's speeches of passion, something very trifling, and something very striking. Richard's debate, whether he should quarrel with himself, is too long continued, but the subsequent exaggeration of his crimes is truly tragical.

V.353

V.iii.204 *King Richard.* Methought, the souls of all that I have murder'd Came to my tent, and every one did threat Tomorrow's vengeance on the head of Richard.

These lines stand with so little propriety at the end of this speech, that I cannot but suspect them to be misplaced.

V.354

[Both J (Yale 8:632) and Lennox (III.169) comment on the improbable aspects of the play.]

HENRY VIII

Prologue.20 and th' opinion that we bring To make that only true we now intend, Will leave us ne'er an understanding friend.

These lines I do not understand, and suspect them of corruption. I believe we may better read thus:

> th' opinion which we bring
> Or make; that only *truth* we now intend.

> V.373

Prologue.25 Be sad, as we would make ye. Think ye see
The very persons of our noble story

This is specious, but the laxity of versification in this prologue, and in the following epilogue, makes it not necessary.

> V.374

I.i.48 *Norfolk.* One, certes, that promises no element
In such a business.

No initiation, no previous practices. "Elements" are first principles of things, or rudiments of knowledge. The word is here applied, not without a *catachresis,* to a person.

> V.378

["Catachresis" is partially quoted in J's *Dictionary* as "when one word is abusively put for another, for want of the proper word" from *Smith's Rhetorick,* i.e., John Smith, *The mysterie of Rhetorique unvail'd* (1657).]

I.i.62 *Norfolk.*   but spider-like
Out of his self drawing web

Thus it stands in the first edition. The later editors, by injudicious correction, have printed,

> Out of his *self-drawn* web.

> V.378

I.i.122 *Buckingham.*   A beggar's book
Out-worths a noble's blood.

That is, the literary qualifications of a bookish beggar are more prized than the high descent of hereditary greatness. This is a contemptuous exclamation very naturally put into the mouth of one of the antient, unlettered, martial nobility.

> V.381

I.i.224 *Buckingham.* I am the shadow of poor Buckingham,
Whose figure ev'n this constant cloud puts on,
By dark'ning my clear sun.

These lines have passed all the editors. Does the reader understand them? By me they are inexplicable, and must be left, I fear, to some happier sagacity.

1765 *Appendix*

I.ii.118 *King.*   This man so compleat,
          Who was enroll'd 'mongst wonders, and when we,
          Almost with list'ning ravish'd, could not find
          His hour of speech, a minute

This sentence is broken and confused, though, with the allowances always to be made to our authour, it may be understood.

V.391

II.i.71 *Buckingham.*   Ye few, that lov'd me,
          And dare be bold to weep for Buckingham,
          His noble friends and fellows, whom to leave
          Is only bitter to him, only dying,
          Go with me, like good angels, to my end:
          And as the long divorce of steel falls on me,
          Make of your prayers one sweet sacrifice,
          And lift my soul to heav'n.—Lead on, o'God's
          name.

These lines are remarkably tender and pathetick.

V.407

II.iii.67 *Anne.* More than my all, is nothing

. . . an hyperbole. Not only my "all is nothing," but if my all were more than it is, it were still nothing.

V.419

III.i.37 *Queen Catharine.*   If your business
          Do seek me out, and that way I am wife in,
          Out with it boldly.

The meaning, whatever it be, is coarsely and unskilfuly expressed.

V.432

III.i.102 *Queen Catharine.* The more shame for you; holy men I
          thought you,
          Upon my soul, two rev'rend cardinal
          virtues,
          But cardinal sins, and hollow hearts, I
          fear you

The distress of Catharine might have kept her from the quibble to which she is irresistibly tempted by the word "cardinal."

V.435

III.ii.355   *Wolsey.* The third day comes a frost, a killing frost,
And when he thinks, good easy man, full surely
His greatness is a ripening, nips his root;
And then he falls, as I do.

[*Warburton:* shoot] The metaphor will not in either reading correspond exactly with nature.

V.452

III.ii.399   *Wolsey.* May have a tomb of orphans' tears wept on him!

The Chancellor is the general guardian of orphans. A "tomb of tears" is very harsh.

V.454

IV.i.9   *2 Gentleman.*   they're ever forward
In celebration of this day with shows,
Pageants, and sights of honour.

Hanmer reads, "these days," but Shakespeare meant "such a day as this," a coronation day. And such is the English idiom, which our authour commonly prefers to grammatical nicety.

V.457

V.iv.36   *Cranmer.* God shall be truly known, and those about her
From her shall read the perfect ways of honour

Our author was at once politick and idle; he resolved to flatter James, but neglected to reduce the whole speech to propriety, or perhaps intended that the lines inserted should be spoken in the action, and omitted in the publication, if any publication ever was in his thoughts.

V.490

KING LEAR

I.i.   There is something of obscurity or inaccuracy in this preparatory scene.

VI.3

I.i.17 *Lear.* Which nor our nature, nor our place, can bear;
              Our potency made good

Lear, who is characterized as hot, heady and violent, is, with very just observation of life, made to entangle himself with vows, upon any sudden provocation to vow revenge, and then to plead the obligation of a vow in defence of implacability.

                                                                    VI.11

I.iii.19 *Gonerill.* Old fools are babes again; and must be us'd
                With checks, as flatteries when they're seen abus'd.

This construction is harsh and ungrammatical; Shakespeare perhaps thought it vitious, and chose to throw away the lines rather than correct them

                                                                    VI.30

I.iv.225 *Fool.* Whoop, Jug

There are in the fool's speeches several passages which seem to be proverbial allusions, perhaps not now to be understood.

                                                                    VI.39

II.iv.1 [Stage Direction] Changes again to the Earl of Glo'ster's
             castle.

It is not very clearly discovered why Lear comes hither. In the foregoing part he sent a letter to Glo'ster, but no hint is given of its contents. He seems to have gone to visit Glo'ster while Cornwall and Regan might prepare to entertain him.

                                                                    VI.61

II.iv.68 *Fool.* All, that follow their noses are led by their eyes, but blind
              men; and there's not a nose among twenty, but can smell
              him that's stinking.

There is in this sentence no clear series of thought.

                                                                    VI.63

II.iv.200 *Cornwall.* Deserv'd much less advancement.

The word "advancement" is ironically used here for "conspicuousness" of punishment; as we now say, "a man is *advanced* to the pillory." We should read,

but his own disorders
Deserv'd much *more* advancement.

VI.70

III.i.7 *Gentleman.* That things might change, or cease, tears his white
hair

The first folio ends the speech at "change, or cease," and begins
again with Kent's question, "But who is with him?" [1.16] The
whole speech is forcible, but too long for the occasion, and properly retrenched.

VI.77

III.i.19 *Kent.* There's division
Although as yet the face of it is cover'd
With mutual cunning, 'twixt Albany and Cornwall.

The true state of this speech cannot from all these notes [Theo-
bald's, Pope's, Warburton's] be discovered. As it now stands it is
collected from two editions: the lines which I have distinguished
by italicks [the following eight] are found in the folio, not in the
quarto; the following [five] lines inclosed in crotchets [brackets]
are in the quarto, not in the folio. So that if the speech be read
with omissions of the italicks, it will stand according to the first
edition; and if the italicks are read, and the lines that follow them
are omitted, it will then stand according to the second. The speech
is now tedious because it is formed by a coalition of both. The
second edition is generally best, and was probably nearest to
Shakespeare's last copy, but in this passage the first is preferable;
for in the folio, the messenger is sent, he knows not why, he knows
not whither. I suppose Shakespeare thought his plot opened
rather too early, and made the alteration to veil the event from
the audience; but trusting too much to himself, and full of a
single purpose, he did not accomodate his new lines to the rest
of the scene.

VI.78

III.ii.48 *Kent.* Man's nature cannot carry
Th' affliction, nor the fear.

So the folio, the later editions read, with the quarto, "force" for
"fear," less elegantly.

VI.82

III.ii.74 *Fool.* "He that has an a little tyny wit,

> With heigh ho, the wind and the rain;
> Must make content with his fortunes fit,
> Though the rain it raineth every day."

I fancy that the second line of this stanza had once a termination that rhymed with the fourth; but I can only fancy it; for both the copies agree. It was once perhaps written,

> With heigh ho, the wind and the rain *in his way*. . . .

Yet I am afraid that all this is chimerical, for the burthen appears again in the song at the end of *Twelfth Night*, and seems to have been an arbitrary supplement, without any reference to the sense of the song.

VI.84

III.iv.26   *Lear.* In, boy, go first. [To the Fool.] You houseless
                  poverty—
                  Nay, get thee in; I'll pray, and then I'll sleep—

These two lines were added in the authour's revision, and are only in the folio. They are very judiciously intended to represent that humility, or tenderness, or neglect of forms, which affliction forces on the mind.

VI.88

III.iv.99   *Edgar.* says suum, mun, nonny, dolphin my boy, boy, Sessy:
                  let him trot by.

Of this passage I can make nothing. I believe it corrupt: for wildness, not nonsense, is the effect of a disordered imagination.

VI.90

III.vi.24   *Edgar. Wantest thou eyes?*
                  At trial, Madam

It may be observed that Edgar, being supposed to be found by chance, and therefore to have no knowledge of the rest, connects not his ideas with those of Lear, but pursues his own train of delirious or fantastic thought. To these words, "At trial, madam?" I think therefore that the name of Lear should be put. The process of the dialogue will support this conjecture. [J is wrong.]

1773:IX.416

III.iv.97   *Kent. Opprest Nature sleeps.*

The lines [from l. 97 to "Lurk, lurk."] inserted from the quarto are in italicks. The omission of them in the folio is certainly faulty: yet I believe the folio is printed from Shakespeare's last revision, carelessly and hastily performed, with more thought of shortening the scenes, than of continuing the action.

VI.99

IV.i.68   *Glo'ster.* That slaves your ordinance

The language of Shakespeare is very licentious, and his words have often meanings remote from the proper and original use.

VI.110

IV.iii.1   [Stage direction] Enter Kent, and a Gentleman.

This scene seems to have been left out only to shorten the play, and is necessary to continue the action. It is extant only in the quarto, being omitted in the first folio.

VI.116

IV.iii.24   *Kent. Made she no verbal question?*

I do not see the impropriety of "verbal question": such pleonasms are common.

VI.117

IV.vi.11   *Edgar.*   How fearful
            And dizzy 'tis to cast one's eyes so low!

He that looks from a precipice finds himself assailed by one great and dreadful image of irresistible destruction. But this overwhelming idea is dissipated and enfeebled from the instant that the mind can restore itself to the observation of particulars, and diffuse its attention to distinct objects. The enumeration of the choughs and crows, the samphire-man and the fishers, counteracts the great effect of the prospect, as it peoples the desert of intermediate vacuity, and stops the mind in the rapidity of its descent through emptiness and horrour.

VI.123

IV.vi.212   *Gentleman.*   The main descry
             Stands on the hourly thought.

The "main" body is "expected" to be "descry'd" every hour. The expression is harsh.

VI.131

V.iii.54   *Edmund.* *At this time,*
                      We sweat and bleed; the friend hath lost his friend;
                      And the best quarrels, in the heat, are curst
                      By those that feel their sharpness.—
                      The question of Cordelia, and her father,
                      Requires a fitter place.

This passage, well worthy of restoration, is omitted in the folio.

VI.146

V.iii.89   *Gonerill.* an interlude!—

This short exclamation of Gonerill is added to the folio edition, I suppose, only to break the speech of Albany, that the exhibition on the stage might be more distinct and intelligible.

VI.148

V.iii.167   *Edgar.* Let's exchange charity.

Our authour by negligence gives his heathens the sentiments and practices of Christianity. In *Hamlet* there is the same solemn act of final reconciliation, but with exact propriety, for the personages are Christians.

Exchange forgiveness with me, noble Hamlet, &c.

VI.151

V.iii.264   *Kent.* Is this the promis'd end?
            Edgar. Or image of that horror—
            Albany. Fall, and cease.

These two exclamations are given to Edgar and Albany in the folio, to animate the dialogue, and employ all the persons on the stage, but they are very obscure.

VI.155

TIMON OF ATHENS

I.i.3   *Poet.* Ay, that's well known.
                But what particular rarity? what so strange,

> Which manifold record not matches? See,
> Magick of bounty! all these spirits thy power
> Hath conjur'd to attend.

I cannot but think that the passage is at present in confusion. The Poet asks a question, and stays not for an answer, nor has his question any apparent drift or consequence.

VI.167

I.i.21   *Poet.* Our poesy is as a gum, which oozes
>   From whence 'tis nourished.

This speech of the poet is very obscure. . . . The images in the comparison are so ill sorted, and the effort so obscurely expressed, that I cannot but think something omitted that connected the last sentence with the former.

VI.168

I.i.30   *Poet.* Admirable? how this grace
>   Speaks his own standing? What a mental power
>   This eye shoots forth?

This sentence seems to me obscure, and however explained, not very forcible.

VI.169

I.i.90   *Painter.* A thousand moral paintings I can shew.

Shakespeare seems to intend in this dialogue to express some competition between the two great arts of imitation. Whatever the poet declares himself to have shewn, the painter thinks he could have shewn better.

1773:VIII.278

I.i.107   *Timon.* 'Tis not enough to help the feeble up,
>   But to support him after.

This though is better expressed by Dr. Madden in his elegy on Archbishop Boulter.

> He thought it mean
> Only to help the poor to beg again.

VI.173

[J told Boswell that "when Dr. Madden came to London, he submitted the work to my castigation; and I remember I blotted a great many lines, and might have blotted many more, without making the poem worse" (*Life,* I.318).]

I.i.234   *Apemantus.* That I had no angry wit to be a lord.

[Warburton: "so hungry a wit"]
The meaning may be, I should hate myself for "patiently enduring to be a lord." This is ill enough expressed. Perhaps some happy change may set it right. I have tried, and can do nothing, yet I cannot heartily concur with Dr. Warburton.

VI.179

I.ii.12   *Timon.* If our betters play at that game, we must not dare
                    T'imitate them. Faults that are rich, are fair.

The whole is a trite and obvious thought, uttered by Timon with a kind of affected modesty.

VI.181

I.ii.105   *Timon.* O joy, e'en made away ere't can be born

Tears being the effect both of joy and grief supplied our authour with an opportunity of conceit which he seldom fails to indulge.

VI.186

I.ii.152   *Lucullus.* My Lord, you take us even at the best.

This answer seems rather to belong to one of the ladies. It was probably only marked "L" in the copy. [J is right.]

VI.189

I.ii.227   *Timon.*   and all the lands thou hast
                    Lie in a pitcht field.
           Alcibiades. I' defiled land, my Lord.

This is the old reading, which apparently depends on a very low quibble. Alcibiades is told, that "his estate lies in a *pitch'd* field." Now "pitch," as Falstaff says, "doth defile." Alcibiades therefore replies, that his estate lies "in defiled land."

VI.192

[*1 Henry IV,* II.iv.412–13, "This pitch (as ancient writers do report) doth defile".]

II.ii.9   *Caphis.* Good even, Varro.

It is observable that this "good evening" is before dinner; for Timon tells Alcibiades, that they will "go forth again as soon as dinner's done," which may prove that by "dinner" our authour meant not the *coena* of ancient times, but the midday's repast. I do not suppose the passage corrupt: such inadvertencies neither authour nor editor can escape.

VI.197

II.ii.46   [Stage direction] Enter Apemantus, and Fool.

I suspect some scene to be lost, in which the entrance of the fool, and the page that follows him, was prepared by some introductory dialogue, and the audience was informed that they were the fool and page of Phrynia, Temandra, or some other courtisan, upon the knowledge of which depends the greater part of the ensuing jocularity.

VI.198

III.iii.28   *Servant.* The devil knew not what he did, when he made man politick

I cannot but think that the negative "not" has intruded into this passage. [J is wrong.]

VI.214

III.iv.66   [Stage direction] Enter Servilius.

It may be observed that Shakespeare has unskilfully filled his Greek story with Roman names.

VI.218

IV.ii.1   [Stage direction] Enter Flavius, with two or three servants.

Nothing contributes more to the exaltation of Timon's character than the zeal and fidelity of his servants. Nothing but real virtue can be honoured by domesticks; nothing but impartial kindness can gain affection from dependants.

VI.231

IV.ii.38   *Flavius.*   strange unusual blood,
          When man's worst sin is, he does too much good.

Of this passage, I suppose, every reader would wish for a correction; but the word [blood], harsh as it is, stands fortified by the rhyme [good], to which, perhaps, it owes its introduction.

VI.232

IV.iii.158   *Timon.*   take the bridge quite away
                          Of him, that his particular to foresee
                          Smells from the gen'ral weal.

The metaphor is apparently incongruous, but the sense is good.

VI.242

IV.iii.252   *Timon.*   Hadst thou, like us from our first swath, proceeded
                        Through sweet degrees that this brief world affords

There is in this speech a sullen haughtiness, and malignant dignity, suitable at once to the lord and the manhater. The impatience with which he bears to have his luxury reproached by one that never had luxury within his reach, is natural and graceful.

VI.248

IV.iii.275   *Timon.*   If thou hadst not been born the worst of men,
                        Thou hadst been knave and flatterer.

Dryden has quoted two verses of Virgil to shew how well he could have written satires. Shakespeare has here given a specimen of the same power by a line bitter beyond all bitterness, in which Timon tells Apemantus, that he had not virtue enough for the vices which he condemns.

VI.249

[A *Discourse Concerning the Original and Progress of Satire* (1693).]

IV.iii.358   *Apemantus.* Thou are the cap of all the fools alive.

The remaining dialogue has more malignity than wit.

VI.252

IV.iii.417   *Timon.*   behold, the earth hath roots;
                             Within this mile break forth an hundred springs
                             Vile olus, et duris hoerentia mora rubetis
                             Pugnantis stomachi composuere famem:
                             Flumine vicino stultus sitit.

I do not suppose these to be imitations, but only to be similar thoughts on similar occasions.

VI.255

[Petronius, Poem 22 (Loeb numbering); the phrase *"duris hoerentia mora rubetis"* was taken by Petronius from Ovid *Metamorphoses* I.105.]

V.iii.4   *Soldier.* Some beast read this; here does not live a man.

There is something elaborately unskilful in the contrivance of sending a soldier, who cannot read, to take the epitaph in wax, only that it may close the play by being read with more solemnity in the last scene.

VI.271

In this tragedy are many passages perplexed, obscure, and probably corrupt, which I have endeavoured to rectify or explain with due diligence; but having only one copy, cannot promise myself that my endeavours will be much applauded.

VI.276

TITUS ANDRONICUS

I.i.167   *Titus.* Lavinia, live; out-live thy father's days,
          And fame's eternal date for virtue's praise!

To "live in fame's date" is, if an allowable, yet a harsh expression. To "outlive" an "eternal date" is, though not philosophical, yet poetical sense. He wishes that her life may be longer than his, and her praise longer than fame.

VI.285

II.ii.1   [Stage direction] Changes to a forest.

The division of the play into acts, which was first made by the editors in 1623, is improper. There is here an interval of action, and here the second act ought to have begun.

VI.301

III.ii.1   [Stage direction] An apartment in Titus' house.

This scene, which does not contribute anything to the action, yet seems to have the same authour with the rest, is omitted in the quarto of 1611, but found in the folio of 1623.

VI.325

All the editors and criticks agree with Mr. Theobald in supposing this play spurious. I see no reason for differing from them; for the colour of the stile is wholly different from that of the other plays, and there is an attempt at regular versification, and artful closes, not always inelegant, yet seldom pleasing. The barbarity of the spectacles, and the general massacre which are here exhibited, can scarcely be considered tolerable to any audience; yet we are told by Jonson, that they were not only borne but praised. That Shakespeare wrote any part, though Theobald declares it "incontestable," I see no reason for believing.

The testimony produced at the beginning of this play, by which it is ascribed to Shakespeare, is by no means equal to the argument against its authenticity, arising from the total difference in conduct, language, and sentiments, by which it stands apart from all the rest. . . . Ravencroft, who, in the reign of Charles II, revised this play, and restored it to the stage, tells us in his preface, from a theatrical tradition I suppose, which in his time might be of sufficient authority, that this play was touched in different parts by Shakespeare, but written by some other poet. I do not find Shakespeare's touches very discernible.

VI.364

[*See* Ben Jonson's introduction to *Bartholomew Fair.*]

MACBETH

I.ii.46   *Lenox.* What haste looks through his eyes?
              So should he look, that seems to speak things strange.

He looks like one that "is big with" something of importance; a metaphor so natural that it is every day used in common discourse.

VI.376

I.iii.146   *Macbeth.*   Come what come may,
                Time and the hour runs through the roughest day.

I suppose every reader is disgusted at the tautology in this passage, "Time and the hour."

VI.387

I.iv.11   *King Duncan.*   There's no art,
                  To find the mind's construction in the face

The "construction of the mind" is, I believe, a phrase peculiar to Shakespeare; it implies the "frame" or "disposition" of the mind, by which it is determined to good or ill.

VI.388

I.iv.23   *Macbeth.*   Your Highness' part
                  Is to receive our duties; and our duties
                  Are to your throne, and state, children and servants;
                  Which do but what they should, by doing every thing,
                  Safe tow'rd your love and honour.

. . . the last line of this speech, which is certainly, as it is now read, unintelligible . . .

VI.389

I.v.46   *Lady Macbeth.*   nor keep peace between
                  Th' effect, and it.

The intent of Lady Macbeth evidently is to wish that no womanish tenderness, or conscientious remorse, may hinder her purpose from proceeding to effect; but neither this, nor indeed any other sense, is expressed by the present reading, and therefore it cannot be doubted that Shakespeare wrote differently, perhaps thus:

            That no compunctious visitings of nature
            Shake my fell purpose, nor keep *pace* between
            Th' effect and it.—

To "keep *pace* between" may signify "to pass between," to "intervene." "Pace" is on many occasions a favourite of Shakespeare. This phrase is indeed not usual in this sense, but was it not its novelty that gave occasion to the present corruption?

VI.394

[J's *Dictionary:* "3. Degree of celerity. To *keep pace,* is not to be left behind."]

I.vi.1   *King Duncan.*   This castle hath a pleasant seat; the air
                  Nimbly and sweetly recommends itself
                  Unto our gentle senses.

"Gentle senses" is very elegant, as it means "placid, calm, composed," and intimates the peaceable delight of a fine day.

VI.396

I.vii.1   *Macbeth.* If it were *done,* when 'tis done, then 'twere well
                        It were done quickly

Of this soliloquy the meaning is not very clear; I have never found the readers of Shakespeare agreeing about it.

VI.398

I.vii.28   [Stage direction] Enter Lady Macbeth.

The arguments by which Lady Macbeth persuades her husband to commit the murder, afford a proof of Shakespeare's knowledge of human nature. She urges the excellence and dignity of courage, a glittering idea which has dazzled mankind from age to age, and animated sometimes the housebreaker, and sometimes the conqueror; but this sophism Macbeth has for ever destroyed by distinguishing true from false fortitude, in a line and a half; of which it may almost be said, that they ought to bestow immortality on the authour, though all his other productions had been lost.

> I dare do all that may become a man,
> Who dares do more, is none.

This topic, which has been always employed with too much success, is used in this scene with peculiar propriety, to a soldier by a woman. Courage is the distinguishing virtue of a soldier, and the reproach of cowardice cannot be borne by any man from a woman, without great impatience.
  She then urges the oaths by which he had bound himself to murder Duncan, another art of sophistry by which men have sometimes deluded their consciences, and persuaded themselves that what would be criminal in others is virtuous in them; this argument Shakespeare, whose plan obliged him to make Macbeth yield, has not confuted, though he might easily have shown that a former obligation could not be vacated by a latter: that obligations laid on us by a higher power, could not be overruled by obligations which we lay upon ourselves.

VI.399

II.i.1   [Stage direction] Macbeth's Castle.

This place is not mark'd in the old edition, nor is it easy to say where this encounter can be. It is not in the "hall," as the editors have all supposed it, for Banquo sees the sky; it is not far from the bedchamber, as the conversation shews: it must be in the inner court of the castle, which Banquo might properly cross in his way to bed. [J is right.]

VI.402

II.i.25   *Macbeth.* If you shall cleave to my consent, when 'tis,
                  It shall make honour for you.

Macbeth expresses his thought with affected obscurity . . .

1773:IV.435

II.i.59   *Macbeth.* And take the present horrour from the time,
                  Which now suits with it.

I believe every one that has attentively read this dreadful soliloquy is disappointed at the conclusion, which, if not wholly unintelligible, is, at least, obscure, nor can be explained into any sense worthy of the authour.

VI.406

II.ii.52   *Lady Macbeth.*   If he do bleed,
                  I'll gild the faces of the grooms withal,
                  For it must seem their guilt.

Could Shakespeare possibly mean to play upon the similitude of "gild" and "guilt"?

VI.409

II.iii.111.   *Macbeth.*   Here, lay Duncan;
                  His silver skin laced with his golden blood

No amendment can be made to this line, of which every word is equally faulty, but by a general blot.

It is not improbable, that Shakespeare put these forced and unnatural metaphors into the mouth of Macbeth as a mark of artifice and dissimulation, to show the difference between the studied language of hypocrisy, and the natural outcries of sudden passion. This whole speech so considered, is a remarkable instance of judgment, as it consists entirely of antithesis and metaphor.

VI.417

II.iii.115   *Macbeth.*   their daggers
                    Unmannerly breech'd with gore.

An "unmannerly dagger," and a "dagger breech'd," or as in some
editions, "breach'd with gore," are expressions not easily to be
understood.

VI.417

III.i.53   *Macbeth.*   There is none but he,
                    Whose being I do fear: and, under him,
                    My genius is rebuk'd; as, it is said,
                    Anthony's was by Caesar. He chid the Sisters

Every boy or girl finds the metre imperfect, but the pedant [Ben-
jamin Heath] comes to its defence with a tribachys or an anapaest,
and sets it right at once by applying to one language the rules of
another. If we may be allowed to change feet, like the old comick
writers, it will not be easy to write a line not metrical.

VI.424

III.i.128   *Macbeth.* I will advise you where to plant yourselves;
                    Acquaint you with the perfect spy o' th' time.

What is meant by "the spy of the time," it will be found difficult
to explain; and therefore sense will be cheaply gained by a slight
alteration ["a perfect spy"].

VI.428

III.iv.1   *Macbeth.* You know your own degrees, sit down:
                    At first and last, the hearty welcome.

As this passage stands, not only the numbers are very imperfect,
but the sense, if any can be found, weak and contemptible.

VI.433

III.iv.60   *Lady Macbeth.*   O proper stuff!
                    This is the very painting of your fear

This speech is rather too long for the circumstances in which it
is spoken. It had begun better at, "Shame itself!"

VI.435

III.iv.1   [Stage direction] Enter Lenox, and another Lord.

As this tragedy, like the rest of Shakespeare's, is perhaps over-
stocked with personages, it is not easy to assign a reason, why a

nameless character should be introduced here, since nothing is said that might not with equal propriety have been put into the mouth of any other disaffected man.

VI.442

IV.i.1   [Stage direction] A dark cave; in the middle, a great cauldron burning. Thunder. Enter the three Witches.

As this is the chief scene of enchantment in the play, it is proper in this place to observe, with how much judgment Shakespeare has selected all the circumstances of his infernal ceremonies, and how exactly he has conformed to common opinions and traditions.

VI.444

IV.iii.2   *Macduff.*   Let us rather
                Hold fast the mortal sword; and, like good men,
                Bestride our down-faln birthdom.

In former editions:

                Let us rather
                Hold fast the mortal sword; and, like good men,
                Bestride our *downfal birthdoom:*—

He who can discover what is meant by him that earnestly exhorts him to "bestride" his "downfal birth-doom," is at liberty to adhere to the present text.

VI.457

IV.iii.195   *Macduff.*   What concern they?
                The gen'ral cause? or is it a fee-grief,
                Due to some single breast?

"Fee-grief." A peculiar sorrow; a grief that hath a single owner. The expression is, at least to our ears, very harsh.

VI.465

V.iii.8   *Macbeth.* And mingle with the English epicures.

The reproach of epicurism, on which Mr. Theobald has bestowed a note, is nothing more than a natural invective uttered by an inhabitant of a barren country, against those who have more opportunities of luxury.

VI.472

V.iv.11   *Malcolm.* For where there is advantage to be given,
                Both more and less have given him the revolt

The impropriety of the expression "advantage to be given," instead of "advantage given," and the disagreeable repetition of the
word "given" in the next line, incline me to read,

> Where there is *a'vantage* to be *gone,*
> Both more and less have given him the revolt.
>   VI.475

V.v.17   *Macbeth.* She should have dy'd hereafter;
                there would have been a time for such a word.

It is a broken speech, in which only part of the thought is
expressed.
                                             VI.476

V.v.23   *Macbeth.* The way to dusty death.

"Dusty" is a very natural epithet.
                                             VI.477

V.v.41   *Macbeth.* I pull in resolution, and begin
                To doubt the equivocation of the friend,
                That lies like truth.

Though this is the reading of all the editions, yet as it is a phrase
without either example, elegance or propriety, it is surely better
to read,

> I *pall* in resolution,—
>   VI.478

CORIOLANUS

I.ii.26   *2 Senator.* Take your commission, hie you to your bands;
                Let us alone to guard Corioli;
                If they set down before's, for the remove
                Bring up your army

[*Warburton:* 'fore they remove]
I do not see the nonsense or impropriety of the old reading. Says

the senator to Aufudius, "Go to your troops, we will garrison
Corioli. If the Romans besiege us, bring up your army *to remove
them*." If any change should be made, I would read,

for *their* remove.

VI.500

I.vi.83   *Coriolanus.*   please you to march,
                  And four shall quickly draw out my command,
                  Which men are best inclin'd.

I cannot but suspect this passage of corruption.

VI.512

I.ix.12   *Lartius.* Here is the steed, we the caparison.

This is an odd encomium. The meaning is, "This man performed
the action, and we only filled up the show."

VI.515

II.i.75   *Menenius.* set up the bloody flag against all patience

That is, declare war against patience. There is not wit enough in
this satire to recompense its grossness.

VI.523

II.ii.25   *2 Officer.*   his ascent is not by such easy degrees as those,
                  who have been supple and courteous to the people,
                  bonnetted

The sense, I think, requires that we should read, "unbonnetted."
Who have risen only by "pulling off their hats" to the people.
"Bonnetted" may relate to "people," but not without harshness.

VI.532

III.iii.127   *Coriolanus.* Have the power still
                  To banish your defenders, 'till at length,
                  Your ignorance, which finds not, till it feels,
                  Making but reservation of your selves,
                  Still your own enemies, deliver you,
                  As most abated captives, to some nation
                  That won you without blows!

It is remarkable, that, among the political maxims of the speculative Harrington, there is one which he might have borrowed from

this speech. "The people," says he, "cannot see, but they can feel." It is not much to the honour of the people, that they have the same character of stupidity from their enemy and their friend. Such was the power of our authour's mind, that he looked through life in all its relations private and civil.

VI.575

[James Harrington, *Political Aphorisms* (1659), No. 5.]

IV.i.7 *Coriolanus.* Fortune's blows,
                When most struck home, being gentle wounded,
                craves
                A noble cunning.

This is the ancient and authentick reading. The modern editors have, for "gentle wounded," silently substituted "gently warded," and Dr. Warburton has explained "gently" by "nobly." It is good to be sure of our authour's words before we go about to explain their meaning.

VI.577

IV.vi.2 *Sicinius.* His remedies are tame i' th' present peace,
                And quietness o' th' people

The meaning, somewhat harshly expressed according to our authour's custom, is this: "We need not fear him," the proper "remedies" against him "are taken," by restoring "peace and quietness."

VI.593

V.iii.206 *Coriolanus.* Ladies, you deserve
                To have a temple built you: all the swords
                In Italy, and her confederate arms,
                Could not have made this peace.

[Warburton suggested the speech be given to Aufidius.]
The speech suits Aufidius justly enough, if it had been written for him; but it may, without impropriety, be spoken by Coriolanus; and, since the copies give it to him, why should we dispossess him?

VI.619

JULIUS CAESAR

I.i.18 *Marullus.* What mean'st thou by that? Mend me, thou saucy
                fellow?

[Theobald gave this speech to Flavius.]
I have replaced Marullus, who might properly enough reply to a
saucy sentence directed to his colleague, and to whom the speech
was probably given, that he might not stand too long unemployed
on the stage.

VII.4

II.ii.36   *Caesar.*   death, a necessary end,
             Will come, when it will come.

This is a sentence derived from the Stoical doctrine of predestination, and is therefore improper in the mouth of Caesar.

VII.39

II.ii.88   *Decius.*   great men shall press
             For tinctures, stains, relicks, and cognisance.

The speech, which is intentionally pompous, is somewhat
confused.

VII.41

ANTONY AND CLEOPATRA

I.i.9   *Philo.* And is become the bellows, and the fan,
          To cool a Gypsy's lust.

In this passage, something seems to be wanting.

VII.106

I.ii.156   *Enobarbus.* Why, Sir, give the gods a thankful sacrifice: when
             it pleaseth their deities to take the wife of a man from him,
             it shews to man the tailors of the earth, comforting therein,
             that when old robes are worn out, there are members to
             make new.

I have printed this after the original, which, though harsh and
obscure, I know not how to amend.

VII.116

I.iv.12   *Lepidus.* His faults in him seem as the spots of heav'n,
             More fiery by night's blackness

If by spots are meant stars, as night has no other fiery spots, the
comparison is forced and harsh, stars having been always sup-

posed to beautify the night; nor do I comprehend what there is in the counter-part of this simile, which answers to night's blackness.
VII.124

I.iv.24 *Caesar.*   we do bear
           So great weight in his lightness.

The word "light" is one of Shakespeare's favourite play-things.
VII.124

I.iv.49 *Messenger.* Make the sea serve them; which they ear

To "ear," is to "plow"; a common metaphor.
VII.126

II.i.1 [Stage direction] Enter Pompey, Menecrates, and Menas.

The persons are so named in the first edition; but I know not why Menecrates appears; Menas can do all without him.
VII.133

II.i.50 *Pompey.* Be't, as our Gods will have't! it only stands
           Our lives upon, to use our strongest hands.
           Come, Menas.

This play is not divided into acts by the authour or first editors, and therefore the present division may be altered at pleasure. I think the first act may be commodiously continued to this place, and the second act opened with the interview of the chief persons, and a change of the state of action. Yet it must be confessed, that it is of small importance, where these unconnected and desultory scenes are interrupted.
VII.136

II.ii.42 *Caesar.* Your wife and brother
            Made wars upon me; and their contestation
            Was theam for you, you were the word of war.

[*Warburton:* theam'd]
I am neither satisfied with the reading nor the emendation; "theam'd" is, I think, a word unauthorised, and very harsh.
VII.139

[There is no verb "to theme" in J's *Dictionary.*]

II.ii.110 *Enobarbus.* Go to then: your considerate stone.

This line is passed by all the editors, as if they understood it, and believed it universally intelligible. I cannot find in it any very obvious, and hardly any possible meaning.

VII.141

II.ii.22   *Soothsayer.* But, near him, thy angel
Becomes a fear

Mr. Upton reads,

Becomes *afear'd,*—

The common reading is more poetical.

VII.148

II.v.1   *Cleopatra.* Give me some musick; musick, moody food
Of us that trade in love

Perhaps here is a poor jest intended between "mood" the mind and "moods" of musick.

VII.150

II.vii.14   *1 Servant.* To be call'd into a huge sphere, and not to be seen to move in't, are the holes where eyes should be, which pitifully disaster the cheeks.

This speech seems to be mutilated; to supply the deficiencies is impossible.

VII.161

II.ii.16   *Enobarbus.* Ho! hearts, tongues, figure, scribes, bards, poets, cannot
Think, speak, cast, write, sing, number, ho!

Not only the tautology of "bards" and "poets," but the want of a correspondent action for the poet, whose business in the next line is only to "number," makes me suspect some fault in this passage, which I know not how to mend.

VII.169

III.vi.69   *Caesar.* Bocchus the King of Lybia, Archelaus

Mr. Upton remarks, that there are some errours in this enumeration of the auxiliary kings; but it is possible that the authour did not much wish to be accurate.

VII.180

III.xiii.126   *Antony.*   O that I were
            Upon the hill of Basan, to out-roar
            The horned herd, for I have savage cause!

It is not without pity and indignation that the reader of this great poet meets so often with this low jest, which is too much a favourite to be left out of either mirth or fury.

VII.198

IV.ii.14   *Enobarbus.* [Aside.] 'Tis one of those odd tricks which
                sorrow shoots
            Out of the mind.

I know not what obscurity the editors find in this passage. "Trick" is here used in the sense in which it is uttered every day by every mouth elegant and vulgar: yet Sir T. Hanmer changes it to "freaks," and Dr. Warburton, in his rage of gallicism, to "traits."

VII.203

IV.ix.15   *Enobarbus.*   Throw my heart
            Against the flint and hardness of my fault,
           Which, being dried with grief, will break to
           powder,
           And finish all foul thoughts.

The pathetick of Shakespeare too often ends in the ridiculous. It is painful to find the gloomy dignity of this noble scene destroyed by the intrusion of a conceit so far-fetched and unaffecting.

VII.214

IV.xv.19   *Antony.* I here importune death a while, untill
            Of many thousand kisses the poor last
           I lay upon thy lips

[Theobald added "Come down" after "lips."]
Mr. Theobald's emendation is received by the succeeding editors; but it seems not necessary that a dialogue so distressful should be nicely regular.

IV.xv.44   *Cleopatra.* That the false huswife Fortune break her wheel

This despicable line has occurred before.

VII.228

[Celia, in *As You Like It,* I.ii.31–32, says "Let us sit and mock the good huswife / Fortune from her wheel."]

V.i.15   *Caesar.* The round world should have shook
                Lions into civil streets, and citizens
                Into their dens

I think here is a line lost, after which it is vain to go in quest. The sense seems to have been this: "The round world should have shook," and this great alteration of the system of things should send "lions into streets, and citizens into dens." There is sense still, but it is harsh and violent.

VII.232

V.ii.4   *Cleopatra.*   it is great
                To do that thing, that ends all other deeds

The speech is abrupt, but perturbation in such a state is surely natural.

VII.235

V.ii.163   *Cleopatra.* Parcel the sum of my disgraces

The word "parcel," in this place, I suspect of being wrong, but know not what to substitute.

VII.244

The most tumid speech in the play [III.vi.42–55] is that which Caesar makes to Octavia.

VII.254

[The third definition of "Tumid" in J's *Dictionary* is "Pompous; boastful; puffy; falsely sublime."]

CYMBELINE

I.i.1   *1 Gentleman.* You do not meet a man, but frowns: our bloods
                No more obey the heavens than our courtiers';
                Still seem, as does the King's.

[*Hanmer: frowns: our looks*] [*Warburton: frowns: our brows*]
    I am now to tell my opinion, which is, that the lines stand as they were originally written, and that a paraphrase, such as the licentious and abrubt expressions of our authour too frequently require, will make emendation unnecessary.

VII.257

I.i.46   *1 Gentleman.*   liv'd in court,
                Which rare it is to do, most prais'd, most lov'd

This encomium is high and artful. To be at once in any great degree "loved" and "praised" is truly "rare."

VII.260

I.i.100   *Posthumus.* And with mine eyes I'll drink the words you send,
Though ink be made of gall.

Shakespeare, even in this poor conceit, has confounded the vegetable "galls" used in ink, with the animal "gall," supposed to be bitter.

VII.262

[The first definition of "gall" in J's *Dictionary* is "The bile; an animal juice remarkable for its supposed bitterness." The seventh and last notes that galls, tumors on trees, are used in making ink.]

I.iv.43   *Posthumus.* I was then a young traveller; rather shun'd to go even with what I heard

This is expressed with a kind of fantastical perplexity.

VII.273

I.v.33   *Cornelius.* I do not like her. She doth think, she has
Strange ling'ring poisons; I do know her spirit,
And will not trust one of her malice with
A drug of such damn'd nature.

This soliloquy is very inartificial. The speaker is under no strong pressure of thought; he is neither resolving, repenting, suspecting, nor deliberating, and yet makes a long speech, to tell himself what himself knows.

VII.279

[J's *Dictionary:* "Inartificial. Contrary to art."]

I.vi.43   *Iachimo.*   Nor i' th' appetite:
Slutt'ry, to such neat excellence oppos'd,
Should make desire vomit emptiness,
Not so allur'd to feed.

"To vomit emptiness" is, in the language of poetry, to feel the convulsions of eructation without plenitude.

VII.284

I.vi.151   *Imogen.* A saucy stranger in his court to mart
As in a Romish stew

The stews of Rome are deservedly censured by the reformed. This is one of many instances in which Shakespeare has mingled the manners of distant ages in this play.

VII.288

II.iii.22   *Song.*   "His steeds to water at those springs
                  On chalic'd flowers that lies"

Hanmer reads

Each chalic'd *flower supplies:*

To escape a false concord. But correctness must not be obtained by such licentious alterations.

It may be noted, that the "cup" of a flower is called *calix,* whence "chalice."

VII.296

[See "Chaliced" in J's *Dictionary:* "*adj.* (from *calix,* Lat. the cup of a flower.) Having a cell or cup; applied by *Shakespeare* to a flower, but now obsolete." The illustrative quotation is from this song in *Cymbeline.*]

II.iii.113   *Cloten.*   The contract you pretend with that base wretch,
                  One, bred of alms, and foster'd with cold dishes,
                  With scraps o' th' court, it is no contract, none

Here Shakespeare has not preserved, with his common nicety, the uniformity of character. The speech of Cloten is rough and harsh, but certainly not the talk of one,

Who can't take two from twenty, for his heart,
And leave eighteen.

VII.301

II.iv.70   *Iachimo.*   Proud Cleopatra, when she met her Roman,
                  And Cyndnus swell'd above the banks, or for
                  The press of boats, or pride.

Shakespeare has no great right to censure poetical exaggeration, of which no poet is more frequently guilty.

VII.305

II.iv.91   *Posthumus.*   This is her honour?

The expression is ironical.

VII.307

III.iii.35   *Arviragus.* What should we speak of,
                           When we are old as you?

This dread of an old age, unsupplied with matter for discourse
and meditation, is a sentiment natural and noble. No state can be
more destitute than that of him who, when the delights of sense
forsake him, has no pleasures of the mind.

VII.320

III.iii.101   *Belarius.* At three and two years old I stole these babes

The latter part of this soliloquy is very inartificial, there being no
particular reason why Belarius should now tell to himself what
he could not know better by telling it.

VII.323

III.iv.159   *Pisanio.*   nay, you must
                    Forget that rarest treasure of your cheek;
                    Exposing it (but, oh, the harder heart!)

[Who does this "harder heart" relate to? Posthumus is not here
talk'd of. Warburton]
I think it very natural to reflect in this distress on the cruelty
of Posthumus.

VII.330

IV.ii.105   *Belarius.*   the snatches in his voice,
                    And burst of speaking, were as his

This is one of our authour's strokes of observation. An abrupt
and tumultuous utterance very frequently accompanies a confused and cloudy understanding.

VII.349

IV.iii.1   [Stage direction] Changes to Cymbeline's palace.

This scene is omitted against all authority by Sir T. Hanmer. It is
indeed of no great use in the progress of the fable, yet it makes
a regular preparation for the next act.

VII.364

IV.iv.9   *Belarius.*   newness
                    Of Cloten's death, we being not known, nor
                    muster'd

> Among the bands, may drive us to a render
> Where we have liv'd

This dialogue is a just representation of the superfluous caution of an old man.

VII.366

V.i.1 *Posthumus.* Yea, bloody cloth, I'll keep thee; for I wisht
. . . .
Let me make men know
More valour in me, than my habits show;
Gods, put the strength o' th' Leonati in me!
To shame the guise o' th' world, I will begin
The fashion. Less without, and more within.

This is a soliloquy of nature, uttered when the effervescence of a mind agitated and perturbed spontaneously and inadvertently discharges itself in words. The speech, throughout all its tenour, if the last conceit be excepted, seems to issue warm from the heart.

VII.368

V.iv.27 *Posthumus.* If you will take this audit, take this life,
And cancel those cold bonds.

This equivocal use of "bonds" is another instance of our authour's infelicity in pathetick speeches.

VII.377

V.v.262 *Imogen.* Think, that you are upon a rock, and now
Throw me again.

In this speech, or in the answer, there is little meaning.

VII.394

This play has many just sentiments, some natural dialogues, and some pleasing scenes, but they are obtained at the expence of much incongruity.

To remark the folly of the fiction, the absurdity of the conduct, the confusion of the names and manners of different times, and the impossibility of the events in any system of life, were to waste criticism upon unresisting imbecillity, upon faults too evident for detection, and too gross for aggravation.

VII.403

TROILUS AND CRESSIDA

I.i.57   *Troilus.*   to whose soft seizure
               The cignet's down is harsh, and spirt of sense
               Hard as the palm of ploughman.

[Warburton: "(spite of sense)"]
I think this passage more forcible and elegant without an alteration.

VII.411

II.ii.88   *Troilus.*   why do you now
               The issue of your proper wisdoms rate,
               And do a deed that fortune never did,
               Beggar that estimation which you priz'd

If I understand this passage, the meaning is, "Why do you by censuring the determination of your own wisdoms, degrade Helen, whom fortune has not yet deprived of her value, or against whom, as the wife of Paris, fortune has not in this war so declared, as to make us value her less." This is very harsh and much strained.

VII.450

III.i.121   *Pandarus.* These lovers cry,
               Oh! oh! they die,
               Yet that, which seems the wound to kill

"To kill the wound," is no very intelligible expression, nor is the measure preserved.

VII.467

III.iii.145   *Ulysses.* Time hath, my Lord, a wallet at his back

This speech is printed in all the modern editions with such deviations from the old copy, as exceed the lawful power of an editor.

VII.484

II.iii.196   *Ulysses.* The providence, that's in a watchful state,
               Knows almost every grain of Pluto's gold

For this elegant line the quarto has only,

> Knows almost every *thing*.

VII.486

IV.v.79   *Aeneas*. Valour and pride excel themselves in Hector

Shakespeare's thought is not exactly deduced. Nicety of expression is not his character.

VII.508

V.iii.27   *Hector*. Life every man holds dear, but the dear man
Holds honour far more precious-dear than life.

"Valuable" man. The modern editions read,

> —*brave* man.

The repetition of the word is in our authour's manner.

VII.532

V.iii.37   *Troilus*. Brother, you have a vice of mercy in you;
Which better fits a lion, than a man.

The traditions and stories of the darker ages abounded with examples of the lion's generosity. Upon the supposition that these acts of clemency were true, Troilus reasons not improperly, that to spare against reason, by mere instinct of pity, became rather a generous beast than a wise man.

VII.533

V.vi.11   *Troilus*. Come both, you cogging Greeks, have at you both.

This epithet has no particular propriety in this place, but the authour had heard of *Graecia Mendax*. [The second definition of "To cog" in J's *Dictionary* is "To obtrude by falsehood."]

VII.541

ROMEO AND JULIET

I.i.176   *Romeo*. Why then, O brawling love! O loving hate!

Of these lines neither the sense nor occasion is very evident. He is not yet in love with an enemy, and to love one and hate another is no such uncommon state, as can deserve all this toil of antithesis.

VIII.12

I.i.184 · *Benvolio.* At thy good heart's oppression.
        Romeo. Why, such is love's transgression.

Such is the consequence of unskilful and mistaken kindness.

   This line is probably mutilated, for being intended to rhyme to the line foregoing, it must have originally been complete in its measure.

VIII.12

I.i.192   *Romeo.* Being vext, a sea nourish'd with lovers' tears

As this line stands single, it is likely that the foregoing or following line that rhym'd to it, is lost.

VIII.13

I.ii.15   *Capulet.* She is the hopeful lady of my earth

"The lady of his earth" is an expression not very intelligible.

VIII.15

I.ii.24   *Capulet.* At my poor house, look to behold this night
            Earth-treading stars that make dark heaven's light.

[This nonsense should be reformed thus,

    Earth-treading stars that make dark *even* light. *Warburton*]

Both the old and the new reading are philosophical nonsense, but they are both, and both equally poetical sense.

VIII.15

I.ii.26   *Capulet.* Such comfort as do lusty young men feel,
            When well-apparel'd April on the heel
            Of limping Winter treads

To say, and to say in pompous words, that a "young man shall feel" as much in an assembly of beauties, "as young men feel in the month of April," is surely to waste sound upon a very poor sentiment.

VIII.16

I.iii.66   *Lady Capulet.* How stands your disposition to be married?
            Juliet. It is an hour that I dream not of.

The modern editors give "it is an *honour.*" I have restored the
genuine word, which is more seemly from a girl to her mother.
"Your," "fire," and such words as are vulgarly uttered in two syllables, are used as dissyllables by Shakespeare. [Only quarto 1 has
"honour."]

VIII.21

II.Prologue.1   [Stage direction] Enter Chorus.

The use of this chorus is not easily discovered, it conduces nothing
to the progress of the play, but relates what is already known, or
what the next scenes will shew; and relates it without adding the
improvement of any moral sentiment.

VIII.35

II.iv.57   *Mercutio.* Nay, I am the very pink of courtesy.
            Romeo. Pink for flower.—
            Mercutio. Right.
            Romeo. Why, then is my pump well flower'd.

Here is a vein of wit too thin to be easily found.

VIII.51

II.iv.132   *Mercutio.* No hare, Sir, unless a hare, Sir in a lenten pye, that
             is something stale and hoar ere it be spent.

The rest is a series of quibbles unworthy of explanation, which
he who does not understand, needs not lament his ignorance.

VIII.53

III.i.176   *Lady Capulet.* He is a kinsman to the Montagues,
             Affection makes him false, he speaks not true

The charge of falshood on Benvolio, though produced at hazard,
is very just. The authour, who seems to intend the character of
Benvolio as good, meant perhaps to shew, how the best minds, in
a state of faction and discord, are detorted to criminal partiality.

VIII.67

III.ii.25   *Juliet.* And pay no worship to the garish sun.

Milton had this speech in his thoughts when he wrote *Il Penseroso*
[l. 122, 141].

Civil night,
Thou sober-suited matron. —Shakespeare
Till civil-suited morn appear. —Milton
Pay no worship to the garish sun. —Shakespeare
Hide me from the day's garish eye. —Milton

VIII.69

III.ii.46   *Juliet.* And that bare vowel, I, shall poison more
                    Than the death-darting eye of cockatrice.

These lines hardly deserve emendation, yet it may be proper to observe, that their meanness has not placed them below the malice of fortune, the two first of them being evidently transposed.

VIII.70

III.v.85   *Juliet.* Ay, Madam, from the reach of these my hands—
                    Would, none but I might venge my cousin's death!

Juliet's equivocations are rather too artful for a mind disturbed by the loss of a new lover.

VIII.86

IV.iii.1   *Juliet.* But, gentle nurse,
                    I pray thee, leave me to myself to-night;
                    For I have need of many orisons

Juliet plays most of her pranks under the appearance of religion; perhaps Shakespeare meant to punish her hypocrisy.

VIII.98

IV.iii.45   *Juliet.* Alas, alas! it is not like, that I
                     So early waking, what with loathsom smells,
                     And shrieks, like mandrake's torn out of the earth,
                     That living mortals, hearing them, run mad.

This speech is confused and inconsequential, according to the disorder of Juliet's mind.

VIII.100

V.i.1   [Stage direction] Enter Romeo.

The acts are here properly enough divided, nor did any better distribution than the editors have already made, occur to me in the perusal of this play; yet it may not be improper to remark,

that in the first folio, and I suppose the foregoing editions are in
the same state, there is no division of the acts, and therefore some
future editor may try, whether any improvement can be made, by
reducing them to a length more equal, or interrupting the action
at more proper intervals.

VIII.108

V.i.3   *Romeo.* My bosom's lord sits lightly on his throne,
                And, all this day, an unaccustom'd spirit
                Lifts me above the ground with cheerful thoughts.

These three lines are very gay and pleasing.

VIII.109

V.iii.229   *Friar Lawrence.* I will be brief, for my short date of breath
                    Is not so long as is a tedious tale.

It is much to be lamented that the poet did not conclude the
dialogue with the action, and avoid a narrative of events which
the audience already knew.

VIII.122

HAMLET

I.i.108   *Bernardo. I think, it be no other; but even so
                    Well may it sort*

These, and all other lines printed in the italick letter, throughout
this play, are omitted in the folio edition of 1623. The omissions
leave the play sometimes better and sometimes worse, and seem
made only for the sake of abbreviation.

VIII.135

I.i.128   *Horatio.* If thou hast any sound, or use of voice,
                Speak to me.

This speech of Horatio to the spectre is very elegant and noble,
and congruous to the common traditions of the causes of
apparitions.

VII.136

I.ii.89   *King Claudius.*   your father lost a father;
                    That father lost, lost his

I do not admire the repetition of the word, but it has so much of our authour's manner, that I find no temptation to recede from the old copies.

VIII.142

I.iv.39–57   *Hamlet.* Angels and ministers of grace defend us!

Hamlet's speech to the apparition of his father seems to me to consist of three parts. When first he sees the spectre, he fortifies himself with an invocation.

Angels and ministers of grace defend us!

As the spectre approaches, he deliberates with himself, and determines, that whatever it be he will venture to address it.

> Be thou a spirit of health, or goblin damn'd,
> Bring with thee airs from heaven, or blasts from hell,
> Be thy intents wicked or charitable,
> Thou coms't in such a questionable shape,
> That I will speak to thee. I'll call thee &c.

This he says while his father is advancing; he then, as he had determined, "speaks to him," and "calls him"— "Hamlet, King, Father, Royal Dane: oh! answer me."

1773:X.179

II.i.111   *Polonius.* It seems, it is as proper to our age
To cast beyond ourselves in our opinions,
As it is common for the younger sort
To lack discretion.

This is not the remark of a weak man. The vice of age is too much suspicion. Men long accustomed to the wiles of life "cast" commonly "beyond themselves," let their cunning go further than reason can attend it. This is always the fault of a little mind, made artful by long commerce with the world.

VIII.177

II.ii.86   *Polonius.* My liege, and Madam, to expostulate
What Majesty should be, what duty is,
Why day is day, night night, and time is time,
Were nothing but to waste night, day, and time.

The commentator [Warburton] makes the character of Polonius, a character only of manners, discriminated by properties superfi-

cial, accidental, and acquired. The poet intended a nobler delineation of a mixed character of manners and of nature.

VIII.181

[*See* my "Characters of Manners: Notes Toward the History of a
Critical Term," *Criticism* 11 (Fall 1969): 343–57.]

III.i.55–87   *Hamlet.* To be, or not to be? That is the question.

Of this celebrated soliloquy, which bursting from a man distracted
with contrariety of desires, and overwhelmed with the magnitude
of his own purposes, is connected rather in the speaker's mind,
than on his tongue, I shall endeavour to discover the train, and
to shew how one sentiment produces another.

VIII.207

III.i.58   *Hamlet.* Or to take arms against a sea of troubles

I know not why there should be so much solicitude about this
metaphor. Shakespeare breaks his metaphors often, and in this
desultory speech there was less need of preserving them.

VIII.208

III.i.69   *Hamlet.* For who would bear the whips and scorns of time

It may be remarked, that Hamlet, in his enumeration of miseries,
forgets, whether properly or not, that he is a prince, and mentions
many evils to which inferior stations only are exposed.

VIII.208

III.i.76   *Hamlet.* To groan and sweat under a weary life

All the old copies have, "to *grunt* and sweat." It is undoubtedly
the true reading, but can scarcely be borne by modern ears.

VIII.209

III.i.88   *Hamlet.* Nymph, in thy orisons
          Be all my sins rememb'red.

This is a touch of nature. Hamlet, at the sight of Ophelia, does
not immediately recollect, that he is to personate madness, but
makes her an address grave and solemn, such as the foregoing
meditation excited in his thoughts.

VIII.209

III.iii.93   *Hamlet.* Then trip him, that his heels may kick at heav'n;
                        And that his soul may be as damn'd and black
                        As hell, whereto it goes.

This speech, in which Hamlet, represented as a virtuous character, is not content with taking blood for blood, but contrives damnation for the man that he would punish, is too horrible to be read or to be uttered.

VIII.236

IV.i.1   [Stage direction] A Royal apartment. Enter King and Queen, with Rosencrantz, and Guildenstern.

This play is printed in the old editions without any separation of the acts. The division is modern and arbitrary; and is here not very happy, for the pause is made at a time when there is more continuity of action than in almost any other of the scenes.

VIII.247

IV.iv.53   *Hamlet.* Rightly to be great
                        Is not to stir without great argument;
                        But greatly to find quarrel in a straw,
                        When honour's at the stake.

The sentiment of Shakespeare is partly just, and partly romantick.

                Rightly to be great,
          Is not to stir without great argument,

is exactly philosophical.

                But greatly to find quarrel in a straw,
                When honour is at stake,

is the idea of a modern hero.

VIII.256

IV.v.84   *King Claudius.* In hugger mugger to inter him

If phraseology is to be changed as words grow uncouth by disuse, or gross by vulgarity, the history of every language will be lost; we shall no longer have the words of any authour; and, as these alterations will often be unskilfully made, we shall in time have very little of his meaning.

VIII.260

[J's *Dictionary:* "Hugger mugger. Secrecy; by-place." There are quotations from Spenser, Samuel Butler and L'Estrange.]

IV.v.158   *Laertes.* Nature is fine in love; and, where 'tis fine,
It sends some precious instance of itself
After the thing it loves.

[Warburton: "is fal'n in love . . . 'tis fal'n"]
These lines are not in the quarto, and might have been omitted in the folio without a great loss, for they are obscure and affected; but, I think, they require no emendation.

VIII.265

IV.vii.19   *King Claudius.* Who, dipping all his faults in their affection,
Would, like the spring that turneth wood to stone,
Convert his gyves to graces.

This simile is neither very seasonable in the deep interest of this conversation, nor very accurately applied. If the "spring" had changed base metals to gold, the thought had been more proper.

VIII.270

V.i.71   *Clown.* "But age, with his stealing steps,
Hath claw'd me in his clutch;
And hath shipped me into the land,
As if I had never been such."

This stanza is evidently corrupted; for it wants what is found in the other two, an alternate rhyme.

VIII.281

V.i.232   *Priest.* Yet here she is allow'd her virgin rites

"Maiden rites" give no certain or definite image. He might have put "maiden wreaths," or "maiden garlands," but he perhaps bestowed no thought upon it, and neither genius nor practice will always supply a hasty writer with the most proper diction.

VIII.287

V.ii.38   *Hamlet.* An earnest conjuration from the King,
As England was his faithful tributary,
As love between them, like the palm, might flourish,
As Peace should still her wheaten garland wear,
And stand a comma 'tween their amities

The expression of our authour is, like many of his phrases, sufficiently constrained and affected, but it is not incapable of explanation. . . . This is not an easy style; but is it not the style of Shakespeare?

VIII.293

V.ii.125   *Horatio.* Is't not possible to understand in another tongue? you will do't, Sir, really.

Of this interrogatory remark the sense is very obscure.

VIII.297

V.ii.185   *Horatio.* This lapwing runs away with the shell on his head.

I see no particular propriety in the image of the lapwing.

VIII.300

V.ii.226   *Hamlet.* Give me your pardon, Sir. I've done you wrong.

I wish Hamlet had made some other defence; it is unsuitable to the character of a good or a brave man, to shelter himself in falsehood.

VIII.303

[Both J (Yale, 8:1011) and Lennox (II.272) note that Hamlet's feigned madness is not essential to the plot but merely "enlivens the Dialogue" (Lennox) or "causes much mirth" (J).]

OTHELLO

I.i.20   *Iago.* One Michael Cassio, a Florentine,
            A fellow almost damn'd in a fair wife

This is one of the passages which must for the present be resigned to corruption and obscurity.

VIII.320

I.ii.2   *Iago.* Yet do I hold it very stuff o' th' conscience

This expression to common readers appears harsh.

VIII.328

[The *locus classicus* of J on "the common reader" is in the life of Thomas Gray, *Lives*, III.441: "In the character of his *Elegy* I rejoice to concur with the common reader; for by the common sense of

readers uncorrupted with literary prejudices, after all the re-
finements of subtilty and the dogmatism of learning, must be
decided all claim to poetical honours."]

I.ii.13   *Iago.* And hath in his effect a voice potential
                As double as the Duke's

All this learning, if it had even been what it endeavours to be
thought, is, in this place, superfluous. There is no ground of supposing, that our author copied or knew the Greek phrase [sug-
gested by Warburton]; nor does it follow, that, because a word has
two senses in one language, the word which in another answers
to one sense, should answer to both. *Manus,* in Latin, signifies
both a "hand" and "troop of soldiers," but we cannot say, that "the
captain marched at the *head* of his *hand*"; or, that "he laid his *troop*
upon his sword." It is not always in books that the meaning is to
be sought of this writer, who was much more acquainted with
naked reason and with living manners.

VIII.329

I.iii.140   *Othello.* Wherein of antres vast, and desarts idle,
                    Rough quarries, rocks, and hills, whose heads touch
                    heav'n

[Pope: desarts wild]
Every mind is liable to absence and inadvertency, else Pope could
never have rejected a word so poetically beautiful. "Idle" is an
epithet used to express the infertility of the chaotic state, in the
Saxon translation of the Pentateuch.

VIII.342

[The fifth definition of "idle" in J's *Dictionary* is "Worthless; barren; not productive of good." This passage in *Othello* is quoted in
exemplification.]

I.iii.344   *Iago.* It was a violent commencement in her, and thou shalt
                see an answerable sequestration.

There seems to be an opposition of terms here intended, which
has been lost in transcription. We may read, "It was a violent
conjunction, and thou shalt see an answerable sequestration"; or,
what seems to me preferable, "It was a violent commencement,
and thou shalt see an answerable *sequel.*"

VIII.352

II.i.160   *Iago.* "To suckle fools, and chronicle small beer."

In this line there seems to be more humour designed, than I can easily discover or explain.

VIII.362

II.i.275 *Iago.*   whose qualification shall come into no true taste again

Whose resentment shall not be so "qualified" or "tempered," as to be "well tested," as not to "retain some bitterness." The phrase is harsh, at least to our ears.

VIII.367

II.i.296 *Iago.*   The thought whereof
        Doth, like a poisonous mineral, gnaw my inwards

This is philosophical. Minerals poisons kill by corrosion.

VIII.367

II.iii.21 *Iago.* What an eye she has? methinks, it sounds a parley to provocation.

The "voice" may "sound" an "alarm" more properly than the "eye" can "sound" a "parley."

VIII.370

III.iii.180 *Othello.* Exchange me for a goat,
            When I shall turn the business of my soul
            To such exsuffolate and blown surmises,
            Matching thy inference.

This odd and far-fetched word was made yet more uncouth in all the editions before Hanmer's, by being printed, "exsufflicate."

VIII.396

[J takes his definition of "exsuffolate" as "*v.a.* (a word peculiar to *Shakespeare.*) To whisper; to buzz in the ear (from the Italian verb *suffolar*)" from Sir Thomas Hanmer's edition of Shakespeare.]

III.iii.352 *Othello.* The spirit-stirring drum, th' ear-piercing fife

"Ear-piercing" is an epithet so eminently adapted to the "fife," and so distinct from the shrillness of the trumpet that it certainly ought not to be changed.

VIII.404

III.iv.103 *Aemilia.* 'Tis not a year, or two, shews us a man

From this line it may be conjectured, that the authour intended
the action of this play to be considered as longer than is marked
by any note of time. Since their arrival at Cyprus, to which they
were hurried on their wedding-night, the fable seems to have been
in one continual progress, nor can I see any vacuity into which a
"year or two," or even a month or two, could be put. On the night
of Othello's arrival, a feast was proclaimed; at that feast Cassio
was degraded, and immediately applies to Desdemona to get him
restored. Iago indeed advises Othello to hold him off a while, but
there is no reason to think, that he has been held off long. A little
longer interval would increase the probability of the story, though
it might violate the rules of the drama. See Act 5. Sc. 2.

VIII.416

III.iv.146   *Desdemona.* For let our finger ake, and it endues
                    Our other healthful members with a sense
                    Of pain

"Endue with a sense of pain," is an expression, which, though it
might be endured, if it were genuine, cannot deserve to be introduced by artifice.

VIII.418

IV.i.118   *Othello.* Do you triumph, Roman, do you triumph?

Othello calls him "Roman" ironically. "Triumph," which was a
Roman ceremony, brought Roman into his thoughts. "What," says
he, "you are now *triumphing* as great as a Roman."

VIII.428

IV.iii.31   *Desdemona.*   I've much ado,
                    But to go hang my head all at one side

This is perhaps the only insertion made in the latter editions
which has improved the play. The rest seem to have been added
for the sake of amplification or of ornament.

VIII.446

V.ii.1   *Othello.* It is the cause, it is the cause, my soul;
                    Let me not name it to you, you chaste stars!
                    It is the cause.

The abruptness of this soliloquy makes it obscure.

VIII.455

V.ii.21   *Othello.* This sorrow's heavenly;
               It strikes, where it doth love.

This tenderness, with which I lament the punishment which jus-
tice compels me to inflict, is a holy passion.
   I wish these two lines could be honestly ejected. It is the fate of
Shakespeare to counteract his own pathos.
                                                                    VIII.456

V.ii.211   *Othello.* That she with Cassio had the act of shame
                A thousand times committed.

This is another passage which seems to suppose a longer space
comprised in the action of this play than the scenes include.
                                                                    VIII.464
[Both J (Yale, 8:1047–48) and Lennox (I.125 and 134) remark
how nearly regular (i.e., adhering to the three dramatic unities)
the play is and on the redeeming features of Othello's character.]

SHENSTONE, WILLIAM

"He used to laugh at Shenstone most unmercifully for not caring
   whether there was anything good to *eat* in the streams he was
   so fond of, 'as if (says Johnson) one could fill one's belly with
   hearing soft murmurs, or looking at rough cascades!'" Piozzi/
   Shaw, p. 147.

J "repeated, with great emotion, Shenstone's lines:

                'Whoe'er has travell'd life's dull round,
                Where'er his stages may have been,
                May sigh to think he still has found
                The warmest welcome at an inn.'"
                                                                    Life, 2:452

[This, despite his generally poor opinion of Shenstone as a poet.]

SHERIDAN, THOMAS (ACTOR)

"his faults seem to be very many, some of natural deficience, and
   some of laborious affectation. . . . His voice when strained is
   unpleasing, and when low is not always heard." *Letters,* I, 130

[J had evidently seen Sheridan in *Cato* and *Richard III*.]

Sheridan's writings on Elocution: "a continual renovation of hope, and an unvaried succession of disappointments." *J Misc.*, 2:1

SHERLOCK, DR. WILLIAM*

Sermons
"Sherlock's style too is very elegant." *Life*, 3:248

"*there* you drink the cup of salvation to the bottom." *J Misc.*, 2:429
[J had Sherlock's *Practical Discourse concerning Death*. Reade, p. 218.]

SIDNEY, SIR PHILIP

"If Sidney had gone . . . the great voyage with Drake, there would probably have been such a narrative as would equally have satisfied the Poet and the Philosopher." *Letters*, 1:243 *See* Language.

SKINNER, STEPHEN*

See Junius, Francis.

SMALRIDGE, DR. GEORGE*

Sermons
His sermons commended . . . *Life*, 3:248

SMITH, ADAM*

Wealth of Nations
"J thought that a man who had never traded himself might write well upon trade, and he said that there was nothing that more

required to be illustrated by philosophy." *P.P.,* 11:137. Cf. *Life,* 2:430 for slightly different wording.

SOCRATES*

Socrates, who had by long observation upon himself and others, discovered the weakness of the strongest, and the dimness of the most enlightened intellect . . . *Adv.* 58, Yale 2:371

SOMERVILLE, WILLIAM

Occasional Poems, Translations, Fables, Tales . . . (1727)
His poem on Addison has this couplet:

> When panting virtue her last efforts made,
> You brought your Clio to the virgin's aid.

"the most elegant compliment that was paid to Addison . . ." *Adv.* 58, Yale, 2:376

In the *Life* of Somerville, of the same couplet: "written with the most exquisite delicacy of praise; exhibits one of those happy strokes seldom attained." *Lives,* 2:319

SOUTH, DR. ROBERT*

He "bid me [Boswell] read South's Sermons on Prayer." *Life,* 2:104

"*South* is one of the best [for style of his sermons], if you except his peculiarities, and his violence, and sometimes coarseness of language." *Life,* 3:248. *See* Barrow, Isaac.
[One volume of South's *Sermons* was marked up for use in compiling the *Dictionary.*]

SPECTATOR

J "observed, that all works which describe manners, require notes in sixty or seventy years or less." *Life,* 2:212.

SPENSER, EDMUND

"Fairies in his [Shakespeare's] time were much in fashion; common tradition had made them familiar, and Spenser's poem had made them great." Yale, 7:160

He "learned to employ his swains on topics of controversy" from Virgil. *Lives*, 3:318 *See* Language.

[J had Spenser's works in six volumes as well as an edition of *The Fairie Queene*. Greene, p. 105.]

STATIUS

Sylvae v. 4 *(Somnus)*
"that pathetic invocation, which he poured out in his waking nights." *Adv.* 39, Yale, 2:349

STEELE, SIR RICHARD

Guardian No. 24
"The Guardian directs one of his pupils 'to think with the wise, but speak with the vulgar.' This is a precept specious enough, but not always practicable." *Idler* 70, Yale, 2:218

STOCKDALE, REV. PERCIVAL*

Translation of Tasso's *Aminta*
"Drs. Johnson and Hawkesworth gave the translator their warm approbation." *Lit. Anecd.*, 8:24

"Stockey . . . is perfectly right; he has defended the cause of Pope with incontrovertible arguments, and with great eloquence" against Joseph Warton's *Essay* on Pope. *Lit. Anecd.*, 8:25n

SURREY, HENRY HOWARD, EARL OF*

J states that his works are "not easy to distinguish from those of Sir *Thomas Wyat* and others." *Hist. Eng. Lang. Dict.* (12ᵛ)

SWIFT, JONATHAN

Celia in *As You Like It* says (III.ii.141)

> "Therefore heaven nature charg'd,
> That one body should be fill'd
> With all graces wide enlarg'd"

and J comments "Perhaps from this passage Swift had his hint of Biddy Floyd" ("On Mrs. Biddy Floyd"). Yale, VII.253

Taylor, Bishop Jeremy*

"Johnson had read much in the works of Bishop Taylor; in his Dutch Thomas á Kempis he has quoted him occasionally in the margin." *J Misc.*, 2:13

See Barrow, Isaac.

[J had two copies of Taylor's *Polemical Discourses* (a short subtitle to a Greek title) and one of his *Ductor Dubitantium, or the Rule of Conscience.* Greene, p. 109.]

Theobald, Lewis

Edition of Shakespeare (1733)

"Some of his amendments are so excellent, that even when he has failed, he ought to be treated with indulgence and respect." *Miscellaneous Observations on the Tragedy of Macbeth* (1745), Yale, 7:8

[The paragraph in which this appears was omitted in J's 1765 *Shakespeare.*]

"Mr. Theobald, if fame be just to his memory, considered learning only as an instrument of gain, and made no further enquiry after his authour's meanings, when once he had notes sufficient to embellish his page with the expected decorations." *Proposals*, Yale, 7:56

"Such critics of Shakespeare as Theobald and Gray [Zachary Grey] perceive matters that eluded Pope and Warburton." Yale, 7:101, n. 5

"I cannot concur [with Warburton] to censure Theobald as a 'critick' very 'unhappy.' He was weak, but he was cautious: finding but little power in his mind, he rarely ventured far under its conduct. His timidity hindered him from daring conjectures, and sometimes hindered him happily." Yale, 8:734

Thirlby, Dr. Styan*

See Jortin, John.

Thomson, James

Britannia

"a kind of poetical invective against the ministry . . ." *Lives*, 3:286

"a man of genius, but not very skilled in the art of composition, to whom however much will be forgiven as an original, that will not be forgiven to an imitator, or successor. . . ." *Letters,* 1:100

TILLOTSON, ARCHBISHOP JOHN*

Sermons
"*there* you drink the cup of salvation to the bottom." *J Misc.,* 2:429.
  See also Barrow, Isaac.

TRAGEDY

See Imagination.

TRANSLATION

"Translations seldom afford just specimens of a language, and best of all those in which a scrupulous and verbal interpretation is endeavoured, because they retain the phraseology and structure of the original tongue." *Hist. Eng. Lang. Dict.* (O2^v).

TYRWHITT, THOMAS*

Of an emendation by Tyrwhitt
"To change an accurate expression for an expression confessedly not accurate, has somewhat of retrogradation." Yale, 7:309

TWISS, RICHARD*

His *Travels Through Portugal and Spain* "are as good as the first book of travels that you will take up. They are as good as those of Keysler or Blainville; nay, as Addison's, if you except the

learning. They are not as good as Brydone's, but they are better than Pococke's." *Life*, 2:345–46. *See also* Chandler, Richard.
[J had a copy of this work. Greene, pp. 111–12.]

UPTON, JAMES*

Critical Observations on Shakespeare 1746, rev., 1748
"his learning only supplies him with absurdities. His derivation of Vice is too ridiculous to be answered." Yale, 8:632

"Upton, who did not easily miss what he desired to find. . . ." Yale, 8:873

"I have seen, in the book of some modern critick, a collection of anomalies, which shew that he has corrupted language by every mode of depravation, but which his admirer has accumulated as a monument of honour." *Pref. to S.*, Yale, 7:91

"Mr. Upton, a man skilled in languages, and acquainted with books, but who seems to have had no great vigour of genius or nicety of taste." *Pref. to S.*, Yale, 7:100–101
[J had Upton's edition of *Dionysius of Halicarnassus*. Reade, p. 218.]

VOLTAIRE

Boswell asked J if he thought Rousseau was as bad a man as Voltaire:
"Why, Sir, it is difficult to settle the proportion of iniquity between them." *Life*, 2:12
[J had Voltaire's history of the age of Louis XIV. Greene, p. 113.]

WALLER, EDMUND

Revision of the last act of Beaumont and Fletcher's *Maid's Tragedy*
"a heap of barbarity . . ." *Diaries, Prayers, Annals*, Yale, 1:191

"The ambiguity of 'deer' and 'dear' [in a passage in *The Comedy of Errors*] is borrowed, poor as it is, by Waller in his poem on the *Ladies Girdle*.

> This was my heav'n's extremest sphere,
> The pale that held my lovely *deer.*" Yale, 7:353

Epitaph on Lady Sedley, ll. 1–4

> Here lies the learned Savil's heir,
> So early wise, and lasting fair;
> That none, except her years they told,
> Thought her a child, or thought her old.

"an elegant compliment . . ." *Ramb.* 143, Yale, 4:400
[J had an edition of Waller's *Poems.* Reade, p. 225.]

WARBURTON, BISHOP WILLIAM

Edition of Shakespeare (1745)
Some examples of J's praise of Warburton's emendations: "judicious and probable," Yale, 7:264; "an acute and excellent conjecture," Yale, 7:394; "acute and judicious," Yale, 7:484; "The sagacity and acuteness of Dr. Warburton," Yale, 8:685. J also criticized Warburton harshly for many emendations.
[J had Warburton's *Shakespeare* as well as his *Divine Legation of Moses,* his *Julian,* and two volumes of his sermons. Greene, p. 115.]

WASSE, JOSEPH*

"I had read in the morning Wasse's Greek trochaics to Bentley. They appeared inelegant and made with difficulty. The Latin Elegy contains only common places harshly expressed so far as I have read, for it is long. They seem to be the verses of a scholar who has no practice of writing." *Life,* 5:445
[JEB attributes this to Christopher Wasse and only notes, "J censures his Greek and Latin verses" (p. 343).]

WATSON, BISHOP RICHARD*

J liked his *Chemical Essays* "very well." *Life,* 4:118

"From this book, he who knows nothing may learn a great deal; and he who knows, will be pleased to find his knowledge recalled to his mind in a manner highly pleasing." *Life,* 4:232, n. 3

[J had the three-volume *Chemical Essays*. Greene, p. 116.]

WHITAKER, REV. JOHN*

History of Manchester
"what large books we have upon it ['the ancient state of Britain']
the whole of which, excepting such parts as are taken from
those old writers, is all a dream, such as Whitaker's 'Manchester.'" *Life*, 3:333
[J owned a copy. Greene, p. 117.]

WRAXALL, SIR NATHANIEL WILLIAM*

*Cursory Remarks . . . in a Tour through . . . the Northern Parts of Eu-
rope* (1775)
"Wraxall is too fond of words." *Letters*, 2:32

XENOPHON*

Cyropaedia
J "apprehended that the delineation of *characters* in the end of
the first book of the 'Retreat of the ten thousand' was the first
instance of the kind that was known." *Life*, 4:31–32.

"In Greek he told me [William Bowles] that the Cyropaedia was
the only author wch he ever fairly red thro', & that was for the
sake of the language." *Life*, 4:524

[J had Xenophon's *Cyropaedia, Hellenica,* and *Anabasis* in Latin.
Greene, p. 119.]

YOUNG, EDWARD

All his poems "evince Fertility of Imagery springing from the
richest soil—as Johnson told me little cultivated." Hester Lynch
Piozzi, *British Synonymy* (1794, 2:371)

"Dr. Johnson despised Young's quantity of common knowledge as
comparatively small" because Young "seemed totally ignorant

of what he called rhepalick or rhopalick verses." *British Synonymy*
2:371–72. Quoted in *Life,* 5:269, n. 3
[Rhopalic. "Applied to verses in which each word contains one
syllable more than the one immediately preceding it." *OED.*]
[J had Young's *Poems on the Last Day.* Reade pp. 226–27.]

Appendix: What Johnson Did Not "Understand" in Shakespeare's Plays

I have set off the word "understand" in my title because I wish to examine those aspects of Shakespeare's work which Johnson admitted to not understanding, using the very word (once he varied by using "comprehend"). He found many passages, words, images "obscure," to be sure, but it is the frankness of his confessing to a lack of understanding in which I am interested. What sorts of things did he not understand? Did others not understand them? Here I have recourse, quite arbitrarily, to the commentary in the Riverside *Shakespeare*, edited by G. Blakemore Evans, et al. (1974), as a vehicle for comparison. I take the notes in order of their appearance in volumes 7 and 8 of the Yale edition of Johnson's works, but give act, scene, and line references (almost entirely the last) to the Riverside edition. Isabella in *Measure for Measure* says, "Heav'n keep your Honour safe!" and Angelo repeats, "Amen: / For I am that way going to temptation, / Where prayers cross" (II.ii.157). Johnson could not understand how "prayers cross," for which Riverside glosses "*cross* = thwart, impede." Johnson's sixth definition of "to cross" in his *Dictionary* is, "To thwart; to impose; to obstruct; to hinder," with six illustrative quotations, none from Shakespeare.

Johnson could not understand the word "clack-dish" in Lucio's words (III.ii.126), "his use was to put a ducket in her clack-dish," which Zachary Grey had explained and which Johnson had added to the appendix in his 1765 *Shakespeare*, i.e., "The beggars, two or three centuries ago, used to proclaim their want by a wooden dish, with a moveable cover, which they clacked, to shew that their vessel was empty."

The Duke says (III.ii.261):

> "He, who the sound of heav'n will hear,
> Should be as holy as severe:
> Pattern in himself to know,
> Grace to stand, and virtue go."

Riverside offers tentative explanations of these lines followed by question marks. Johnson, however, had suggested emending two words.

The Clown in *As You Like It* says (II.iv.55), "all is mortal in nature, so is all nature in love mortal in folly." Johnson thought, wrongly, that "mortal," from "mort," a great quantity, obtained in these words and was part of a pun. Nor did he understand the Clown's reference to

201

"dulcet diseases" (V.iv.61) and would read "discourses" for "diseases," although Riverside gives "pleasing discomfort" for the words. Johnson defines "dulcet" in his *Dictionary* as "sweet to the taste" and "sweet to the ear."

The Clown says (III.ii.37), "Truly, thou art damn'd, like an ill-rosted egg all on one side," of which simile Johnson did not "fully comprehend the meaning." Riverside: "ruined, like an egg roasted in the ashes that when opened proves to be done on one side but still raw on the other."

Biron in *Love's Labour's Lost* mentions (V.ii.543) "A bare throw at novum," and Johnson again confessed, "this passage I do not understand." Riverside explains: "except for a lucky throw of the dice in the game of novum (from Latin *novem*, 'nine'), played by five players and having nine and five as its principal throws. The quibble here is on the presentation of nine characters by five players."

Hermione in *The Winter's Tale* says (III.ii.48):

> "since he came
> With that encounter so incurrent I
> Have strain'd to appear thus"

Johnson proposed "stain'd" and "have I," but Riverside found no difficulties. The Clown in the same play says (IV.iv.742), "Advocate's the court-word for a pheasant." William Warburton's note, quoted by Johnson, reads, "This satire on the bribery of the courts, not unpleasant," to which Johnson responded, "This satire or this pleasantry, I can confess myself not well to understand." Riverside notes that "A pheasant or other bird was often given as a bribe to a judge."

Johnson had trouble understanding many of the lines given to Shakespeare's clowns. He of *Twelfth Night* says (II.ii.26), "I did impeticos thy gratility," and Johnson confessed, "There is yet much in this dialogue which I do not understand." Hence, when Sir Toby invokes "Peg-a-Ramsey" (II.iii.76), Johnson had again to admit not understanding. Riverside is uncertain on "impeticos," sees "gratility" as a diminutive of "gratuity" and identifies "Peg-a-Ramsey" as "A term of contempt, alluding to a character in a coarse ballad." Sir Toby says (II.v.190), "Shall I play my freedom at tray-trip," which Riverside identifies as a game at dice, something of which Johnson would seem to have been innocent. As will further be seen, Johnson's knowledge of vulgar language was fairly limited.

Falstaff of *The Merry Wives of Windsor* says (V.v.25), "I will keep my sides to myself, my shoulders for the fellow of this walk." Johnson could not identify the "fellow of this walk" nor could he understand why Falstaff keeps his shoulders for him. Riverside sees no difficulty and explicates (p. 319). In *Much Ado About Nothing*, beginning with Benedick's rejoinder, "Like the old tale, my lord, it is not so, nor 'twas not so, but indeed, God forbid it should be so," to Claudio's, "If this were so, so were it uttered" (I.i.215–18), Johnson had to admit that "This and the next three speeches (ll.219–21) spoken by Claudio, Don Pedro, and Claudio have reference to the "old tale," which Riverside explains: "Apparently some form of the Bluebeard story. In an eighteenth-century version cited by Furness a lady who has discovered the bodies of the victims describes her experience, under the fiction that she is recalling a dream, and at intervals the murderer, who is among the listeners, interjects the words here quoted," i.e., the latter part of Benedick's rejoinder, set off by marks of quotation in the Riverside text. Small wonder that Johnson did not understand and attempted an emendation. In the same play, Benedick says (II.i.207), "It is the base (tho' bitter) disposition of Beatrice, that puts the world into her person, and so gives me out." Johnson comments, "I do not understand how 'base' and 'bitter' are inconsistent, or why what is 'bitter' should not be 'base.'" Riverside is uncertain of the meaning of the unamended text, adding "The locution is not very natural, and Johnson emended it to *base, the bitter*," presumably with approval.

Helena of *All's Well That Ends Well* says (I.i.203), "is a virtue of a good wing, and I like the wear well," and Johnson was again nonplussed. Riverside explains that it means nothing more than "characteristic excellence of a good wing, i.e. rapid flight."

Johnson did not understand Prince Henry's allusion to "the melancholy of Moor-ditch" in *1 Henry IV* (I.ii.77). Riverside identifies Moor-ditch, but does not explain why it is associated with melancholy. Recourse to the Variorum edition reveals that the best explanation is that Moor-ditch was invoked by reason of alliteration, as in a preceding line [melancholy] as "an old lion, or lover's lute." And when Falstaff in the same play says (III.iii.,12), "There's no more faith in thee than in a stew'd prune; no more truth in thee than a drawn fox," Johnson comments, "The propriety of these similes I am not sure I fully understand." He offered a tasteless prune for one and an extenerated fox for the other, ignorant, because of his lack of familiarity with gutter language, that a "stew'd prune" was a bawd. A drawn fox, according to Riverside, was "one out of its hole (and seeking to trick its pursuers)." So, too, it was with Falstaff's words in *2 Henry IV* (II.iv.244), "he plays at quoits well, and eats conger and fennel, and drinks off candles' ends for flap dragons," none of which "qualifications" Johnson could understand. George Steevens, Johnson's collaborator in the 1773 *Shakespeare*, cleared up the last qualification: "A 'flap-dragon' is some small combustible body, fired at one end, and put afloat in a glass of liquor. It is an act of topers' dexterity to toss off the glass in such a manner as to prevent the 'flap-dragon' from doing mischief."

The words "to rive," used of artillery, occur in *1 Henry VI* (IV.ii.28), and Johnson, puzzled by the verb, proposed "to drive." Riverside explains "rive" as "cause to burst, discharge." Curiously enough, Johnson quotes the same passage in Shakespeare in his *Dictionary* as a secondary definition of "to rive," i.e., "for *derive* or *direct*," part of the primary definition being "to force into disruption." King Richard III and Buck-ingham engage in some word play revolving about the clock and a "Jack" that "keeps the stroke" (*Richard III*, IV.ii.115), and Johnson, admitting that he did not believe the passage "corrupted," could not understand it. Riverside: "The general sense is that Buckingham . . . is like a Jack (the manikin in old clocks that strikes the bell) poised for action." *OED* corroborates; see "Jack of the Clock" under number 37. Johnson's very second note on *Henry VIII* concerns the prologue's "and th' opinion that we bring / To make that only true we now intend" (20), which he sus-pected of corruption and for the second line of which he suggested an emendation. The passage is neither corrupt nor in need of emendation, Riverside offering, for lines 20–21, "i.e., our intention of presenting a veracious account." Still in *Henry VIII*, A porter refers to (V.iii.62) "the tribulation of Tower-hill or the limbs of Limehouse." Johnson suspected "the Tribulation" to have been "a puritanical meeting-house" but con-fessed ignorance of "the limbs of Limehouse." "Tribulation," according to Riverside, is a "gang of rowdies" and Limehouse was a "disreputable dock district before the Tower," hence the conjunction of Tower-hill and Limehouse. Again, an aspect of contemporary language with which Johnson, the lexicographer, was unfamiliar.

Unfortunately for Johnson, *King Lear*, the next play in his edition, has its fair share of unfamiliar language and allusions, the first of which (II.ii.9), comes with Kent's, "If I had thee in Lipsbury pinfold, I would make thee care for me." Johnson was at his most uncertain: "The allu-sion *which seems to be* contained in this line I do not understand" (my emphasis). He also confessed he did not know what a "three-suited knave" was and for "one-trunk inheriting slave" he suggested "a wearer of old cast-off cloaths, an inheritor of torn breeches." Riverside explains one allusion as "having three suits (a servant's annual allowance)" and the other as "owning no more than will fit into a single trunk (*in-herit* = possess)." One of the definitions of "to inherit" in Johnson's *Dic-tionary* is "to possess" and he quotes a passage from *Titus Andronicus* in exemplification. As for "Lipsbury pinfold," a "pinfold is a pound for stray animals; Lipsbury is an invented place-name (Lipville) presumably meaning 'mouth'; i.e. if I had you between my teeth." All this was obvi-ously beyond Johnson's ken. Kent calls the Steward (II.ii.64), "Thou whoreson zed! thou unnecessary letter," and Johnson could "not well understand how a man is reproached by being called 'zed' nor how 'Z' is an unnecessary letter." He suggested that "zed" be emended to "C (for cuckold)" because "one of its two sounds being represented by S, and one by K." Riverside states that "the letter Z is unnecessary because its sound could easily be represented by S." Johnson was nearly on the right track. But he could not "critically understand" Lear's reference to "tender hefted nature" (II.iv.171), although he acknowledged that "the general meaning" of the word was "plain." The word is hyphenated in the Riverside text and explained as "moved by a tender nature, lovingly

inclined." Here one wonders why Johnson could not "critically" understand the word in its context, for there seems no difficulty in the whole
of Lear's speech of which the line in question was a part.

Alcibiades, in *Timon of Athens* (III.v.21) says "And with such sober and
unnoted passion / He did behave his anger ere 'twas spent." Johnson
noted that the "original copy reads not 'behave' but 'behove,'" but admitted to not understanding either reading. He essayed a "daring conjecture," i.e., "He did *behold* his adversary *shent*," [destroyed] emending in
two places. Riverside defines "behove" as "make seemly," noting that
"Most editions adopt Rowe's emendation *behave*, i.e. manage, regulate."
Warburton had glossed "curb, manage," which Johnson, who recorded
it, ignores. Johnson defines "behove" in his *Dictionary* as "To be fit, to be
meet," which definition might have helped him here. He emended again,
not "easily" understanding Sicinius, in *Coriolanus*, who says (III.iii.17),
"Insisting on the old prerogative / And power i' th' truth o' the cause."
He substituted "O'er" for "i," but Riverside sees no problem, merely
noting that "truth" here meant "justice." Sicinius later says (IV.vi.2) "His
remedies are tame, the present peace," altered to "His remedies are
tame i' th' present peace" and so printed in Johnson's edition. Johnson,
however, could not understand "either line" and emended "tame" to
"ta'en," i.e., "taken," again unnecessarily as "remedies" are "means of
redress" (Riverside).

Caesar, in the play that bears his name, says (III.i.39) "And turn pre-
ordinance and first decree / Into the lane of children," which Johnson
and, presumably, many others could not understand. He proposed "law"
for "lane," which "pre-ordinance" and "decree" of the preceding line
would seem to demand. The Riverside text reads "Into the [law] of
children" and credits Johnson with this "conjecture." Warburton had
offered a recondite explanation of Cleopatra's "Oh, my oblivion is a
very Antony" (I.iii.90) which Johnson did not understand, suggesting
"remembrance" for "oblivion," despite the fact that the first definition of
"oblivion" in his *Dictionary*, "Forgetfulness," is exemplified by quotations
from *Troilus and Cressida* and *The Taming of the Shrew.* Cleopatra says
(II.v.102), "Oh, that this fault should make a knave of thee, / Thou art
not what thou'rt sure of! Get thee hence," which Johnson did not find
"easily" understandable. He rejected an emendation by Sir Thomas
Hanmer and suggested that the second line consisted "only of abrupt
starts." Riverside merely explicates "what thou'rt sure of," "i.e. as bad as
the news you bear." Scarus refers to Cleopatra as "Yon ribaudred nag
of Egypt" (III.x.10), but the text which Johnson received and printed
had "ribauld." He said he could not understand the word in the original
text, although it was not a long leap to "ribald" meaning lewd," as Riverside points out, noting that it was not found elsewhere. Enobarbus says
(III.xiii.9) "he being / The meered question," and Johnson wrote, "The
'meered' question is a term I do not understand" and offered "mooted."

Riverside explicates that the "meered question" is the "sole point at issue."

The formula varied slightly at Troilus's words (II.ii.88), "why do you now / The issue of your proper wisdoms rate, / And do a deed that fortune never did, / Beggar that estimation which you priz'd," for Johnson comments, "If I understand this passage, the meaning is," followed by his explanation, but concluding with an admission that "This is very harsh, and much strained." Despite his reservations, Johnson was right, as recourse to Riverside (p. 462) will demonstrate. Paris says (III.i.80), "I'll lay my life, with my disposer Cressida," and Johnson could not understand "disposer" nor could he "know what to substitute in its place." Riverside notes: "Meaning uncertain; probably a courtly turn of phrase meaning that he was always at her disposal or command." Johnson was not, therefore, alone in his uncertainty. And although Johnson was not unfamiliar with prostitutes, he did not know that "loving quails" in Agamemnon's "one that loves quails" (V.i.51–52) were prostitutes in the slang of the day. Troilus's "If there be rule in unity itself" (V.ii.141) caused Johnson to suggest "purity" or "verity" for "unity," although he conceded that there might be meaning in the unamended text. He suggested that the meaning was "if it be a *rule* that *one is one*," anticipating Riverside's, "if one is one and not dividable into two." Eventually, then, despite his original confession of not understanding, he did understand the line. Iachimo, of *Cymbeline*, says (I.vi.35) "the twinn'd stones / Upon the number'd beach." Johnson did not know "how to regulate this passage" and could not understand "twinn'd stones," while Riverside gives what would seem to be a perfectly obvious gloss, i.e., "looking exactly alike."

Capulet says (I.ii.32), "Which on more view of many, mine, being one, / May stand in number, tho' in reck'ning none," and Johnson could not understand the first of the two lines and tried an emendation. Riverside finds the passage "obscure" and states that it "seems to mean," giving an involved explanation. Again Johnson was not alone in his non-understanding. And he was again puzzled by what turns out to be a nonce word, for when Juliet's nurse refers to "skains mates" (II.iv.153) he supposed "that 'skains' was some low play, and 'skains-mate,' a companion in such play. Riverside has it a "derogatory form not occurring elsewhere." *OED*, quoting the Nurse, has "*Obs.* (Origin and exact meaning uncertain)," but gives "skain" as a variant of "skein," the primary meaning of which is "A quantity of thread or yarn, wound to a certain length upon a reel, and usually put up in a kind of loose knot." Johnson was wrong in his conjecture, but it is not beyond the bounds of possibility that "skains-mates" were women who worked together at winding a quantity of thread or yarn and then putting it up in a kind of loose knot. Evidently the Nurse considered it a low form of employment, not one fitting her position.

At the juncture (II.ii.322) where Hamlet says "the humorous man, shall end his part in peace," the folio text continues with "the clown shall make those laugh whose lungs are tickled o' th' sere." Johnson comments, "This passage I have omitted, for the same reason, I suppose, as the other editors. I do not understand it." Riverside explains "tickled o' th' sere" as "easily made to laugh (literally, describing a gun that goes off easily; *sere* = a catch in the gunlock; *tickle* = easily affected, highly sensitive to stimulus)." "Sere" in this sense is absent from Johnson's *Dictionary*. When Hamlet says (IV.ii.27), "The body is with the King, but the King is not with the body," Johnson could not "comprehend" this answer and, as he was wont, suggested an emendation. Riverside is tentative: "Possibly alluding to the legal fiction that the king's dignity is separate from his mortal body." And Johnson, as were so many others, was baffled by the terms of the wager in the dueling scene in *Hamlet*, writing that he could not "understand" one point of the wager nor "comprehend" the other, and concluding "The passage is of no importance; it is sufficient that there was a wager." Riverside repeats that the latter part of the wager is "Not satisfactorily explained despite much discussion." Osric says (V.ii.165) "The King, Sir, hath laid in a dozen passes between you and him [Laertes], he shall not exceed you three hits; he hath laid on twelve for nine", and George Steevens also gave up:

> As three or four complete pages would scarcely hold the remarks already printed, together with those which have lately been communicated to me in MSS. on this very unimportant passage [so Johnson], I shall avoid both partiality and tediousness, by the omission of them all. —I therefore leave the condition of this wager to be adjusted by the members of Brookes's, or the Jockey-Club at Newmarket, who on such subjects may prove the most enlightened commentators, and must successfully bestir themselves in the cold unpoetick dabble of calculation. (1793, 15:337)

Generations of Shakespeareans tried to understand the wager; Johnson frankly and unashamedly confessed not to understand or to comprehend.

Finally, one passage in *Othello*. Cassio says (II.1.48), "His bark is stoutly timber'd; and his pilot / Of very expert and approv'd allowance; / Therefore my hopes, not surfeited to death, / Stand in bold cure." Johnson suggested as many as three different emendations in the last two lines, the lines he did not understand. Riverside explains those two lines thus: "since I have not had to indulge my hopes so long that they are near death, I am confident that they will be fulfilled."

What, then, does one conclude from the forty-four notes in which Johnson confesses not understanding? First, one is struck, as I noted above, with the frankness with which he unambiguously and forthrightly admitted his inability to understand. Most of the time where he did not understand, he suggested an emendation. In his preface to the edition of Shakespeare Johnson wrote, "As I practiced conjecture more, I learned to trust it less; and after I had printed a few plays, resolved to insert none of my own readings in the text." Hence, he compares very well with most other eighteenth-century editors of Shakespeare, but it must not be forgotten that he suggested many emendations although he did not advance them into the text. Recourse to the index in volume 8 of the Yale edition of Johnson's works reveals that he offered emendations in 462 notes, in a number of which he suggested more than one emendation. Johnson is revealed to have been relatively unfamiliar with slang and the language of the gutter, despite the category of "low" words in his *Dictionary*. He might, incidentally, have profited from turning to the *Dictionary* for help in understanding two or three of the notes which gave him difficulty. In a small number of these notes he was on the side of the angels, two of his suggested emendations having gained wide approval. In others of his notes his difficulties have been shared by future commentators, some of the passages causing the difficulties still either unresolved or tentatively explained. All in all, in sum, he comes off fairly well in this small corpus of his notes.

Index

I have practiced economies in this index as I have in others in the past. The abbreviations for Shakespeare's plays are those given in the *Shakespeare Quarterly* Bibliography, volume 6, number 6 (1985), pp. 691–92. A number of entries for the plays are for pages where the titles are not named but easily recognizable characters are. Articles in the names of the works indexed are omitted; many titles, abbreviated without benefit of ellipses, are still identifiable by author and/or first words of those titles. Names of works abbreviated in the index are given in full in the text, i.e. Boswell's *Letter to the People of Scotland* will appear as *Letter* in the index. Some names are abbreviated: Chas., Geo., Robt., Thos., Wm. References to Boswell's *Life* of J are not listed, as they appear on virtually every page, although not in the sections on Shakespeare. I have not listed mere references to Shakespeare or to Johnson. The various parts of Johnson's *Dictionary*, as well as the Plan of the *Dictionary*, are all listed under Johnson, *Dictionary*. There are no index listings for the introduction. Easily understandable abbreviations are used in titles and in some other entries.

* = Not in JEB

209